CONNECTIONS

Cuba
Liz Lochhead

Dog House
Gina Moxley

Liz Lochhead's plays include *Quelques Fleurs, Blood and Ice, Dracula, The Big Picture, The Magic Island* (an adaptation of *The Tempest*, staged at the Unicorn Children's Theatre), *Shanghai'ed, Tartuffe* (a rhyming Scots translation of Molière's masterpiece), a translation/adaptation of the *York Mystery Plays* and the award-winning *Mary Queen of Scots Got Her Head Chopped Off*. She also writes for film, TV and radio. Her most recent poetry publication is in *Penguin Modern Poets Four*.

Gina Moxley is both a writer and an actor. *Danti-Dan* her first play, was commissioned by Rough Magic and was produced in Dublin in 1995. She wrote *Toupees and Snare Drums* for the Abbey Theatre with CoisCéim Dance Theatre, and *Tea Set* for Fishamble's Y2K festival. In 1995 she received a literature bursary from the Irish Arts Council and was winner of the Stewart Parker Trust Award for New Writers in the Theatre in 1996.

Cuba

LIZ LOCHHEAD

Dog House

GINA MOXLEY

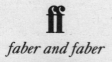

faber and faber

First published in this edition 2001
by Faber and Faber Limited
3 Queen Square London WC1N3AU
Published in the United States by Faber and Faber, Inc.,
an affiliate of Farrar, Straus and Giroux, New York
Cuba and *Dog House* was first published in *New Connections* in 1997

Typeset by Parker Typesetting Service, Leicester
Printed in England by Mackays of Chatham PLC, Chatham, Kent

A CIP record for this book
is available from the British Library

ISBN 0–571–20686–7 (Faber edn)
ISBN 0–7487–4291–3 (Stanley Thornes edn)

2 4 6 8 10 9 7 5 3 1

Contents

Foreword

The plays in this series were generated through a unique and epic project initiated by the Royal National Theatre, London, and funded by BT.

For many years the Education Department at the RNT had been receiving calls from youth theatre companies and schools asking us to recommend scripts for them to perform. They were looking for contemporary, sophisticated, unpatronising scripts with great plots and storylines, where the characters would fit the age range of the young people playing them. At that time, there weren't many plays written for the 11-to-19 age group. So we decided to approach the best writing talent around and ask them to write short plays specifically for young people.

In two-year cycles over a period of six years, we created a portfolio of new plays and invited 150 schools and youth theatres to choose the one that most excited them. We then invited the participants to come on a weekend retreat and work through the script with the writer before producing the play in their home venue. Some of those productions were then invited to one of ten festivals at professional theatres throughout the UK. Each two-year cycle culminated in a summer festival at the Royal National Theatre, where the stages, back-stage areas and foyers were ablaze with youthful energy and creativity.

But the story doesn't end there. As we've discovered, the UK isn't alone in demanding fantastic new scripts for the youth market. A fourth cycle is already under way and this time the portfolio will include more contributions from overseas. As long as there's a need, we will continue to commission challenging work to feed the intelligence, imagination and ingenuity of young people and the adults with whom they work.

Suzy Graham-Adriani
Royal National Theatre
July 2000

For more information on the writers and the work involved on the BT/National Connections project, visit: www.nt-online.org

CUBA

Liz Lochhead

Characters

B., the narrator, late forties, but appears ageless
Barbara Proctor, fourteen
Bernadette Griggs, fourteen
Dr Proctor, early forties
Mrs Proctor, early forties
Mr Griggs, early forties
Mrs Griggs, early forties
Mr Shaw, late twenties
Miss Arthur, mid-twenties
Mr Cairncross, forties
Old Prentiss, fifties/sixties
Eleanor/Girl Messenger, fourteen
Pamela, fourteen
Sandra, fourteen
Marianne, fourteen
Susan, fourteen
Linda, fourteen
Maureen, fourteen
Beth, fourteen
Jean-Ann, fourteen
Extra members of Chorus, if desired. Also two Chorus
members to play two Cleaners

Note: The pieces of dialogue in square brackets are
(Scottish) alternatives to the standard English text. These
are included to encourage any company performing the
play to similarly, here or elsewhere, localize the speech at
their own discretion. The events should sound as though
they happened in a Grammar School in *your* town in
1962.

*The narrator, B., is 'sorting through' in her parents' house
after the death of her (long-widowed) mother. 'Sadness
acting' of any sort is strictly to be avoided though. She is
flooded with memory and this is likely to be exhilarating
beyond all grief. B. drags a big dusty old cardboard box
across centre stage, stops, wipes her dusty hands on the
seat of her trousers, picks out a dusty old book, blows,
registers that it is a copy of* Palgrave's Golden Treasury, *sees that tucked into it, though much bigger, is a real
large-size school photograph – we only see the back of it –
which she holds in front of her, perusing, as behind her,
central, lights come up on a still tableau . . .*

*The Chorus in the form of that school photograph of a
grammar school form of fourteen/fifteen-year-old pupils
all girls, circa 1962 – that is, in the days of obligatory
school uniform and two or three years before hemlines
even thought of climbing towards the idea of the miniskirt.
Among them are Barbara and Bernadette as well as the
Chorus – made up of as many girls as the director wishes,
but the minimum number is nine more, the sum of those
individual characters (Eleanor, Pamela, Sandra, Marianne,
Susan, Linda, Maureen, Beth, Jean-Ann, the classmates we
will meet later, and then there are Mr Prentiss (or Mrs
Prentiss, whichever the director may choose) and Miss
Arthur and Mr Shaw on either side of Mr Cairncross in
the middle of the back row.*

The girls of the Chorus begin to recite by rote.

Chorus
I remember, I remember the house where I was born,

The little window where the sun came peeping in at
morn.
It never came a wink too soon, or brought too long a day
But now I often wish the night had borne my breath
away . . .

B. That's never us. It is though! There she is, and there's
me. Back row, to the left. There we are. Barbara and
Bernadette, Berni and Barb. *Un*believable.

*Barbara and Bernadette, summoned ghosts, split, one
each side, from their places in the photograph and
move slowly down midstage to the right and left as B.
sinks to her knees by the box, puts down the
photograph and peruses the dusty old book, smiling.
Speaks out clearly and evenly. She is well beyond tears
in all this.*

Palgrave's Golden Treasury . . . Every home should have
one. I didn't know we did . . . Not a lot of poetry round
our house, not that I can remember, not when I was
growing up. Maybe I should take it back to Sarah, little
souvenir of your Grandma, mmm? Must've been Mum's
. . . Oh look, a school prize!

She was so proud of you, Sairey, when you were born
that was the first thing I did she ever really approved of.
You two always got on like a house on fire. I know how
much you're going to miss her. I'll miss her. Oh, Mum, I
miss you so much. Where are you?

*B. hugs her arms around her stomach and rocks a beat
or two back and forward. Stops and pep-talks herself.*

Come on, come on, B. The sooner you get this done the
sooner you can go home. (*She picks up the photograph.*)
Take this? This'll make Will laugh. Wonder if my lot
would recognize me? Which one's Mum? Can you see
me? Which one am I? That's us, Bernadette and
Barbara, Barbara and Bernadette. Inseparable. Hah! So

they said. So we thought. Thing is we came from very different families.

In their two tight spots on either side of the stage, some more summoned ghosts, Barbara's family, the Proctors, Mum and Dad, and Bernadette's, the Griggses, Mum and Dad, appear very slowly, like almost identical tableaux coming to life. Different families? At first sight they could not be more similar. The Mums – both in party dresses of 1962 (ideally one a shiny sheath and the other a taffeta ballerina-length full-skirted effort) and both with faded flowery aprons on top – are ironing, in unison, and the Dads sit on armchairs behind newspapers.

Barbara and Bernadette, sobbing, heads down in shame as at the very end of the play, approach their home spaces.

In their separate homes, simultaneously, the Mums put down their irons and look fondly and sympathetically at their daughters. They too are in their very-end-of-the-play state.

Mrs Proctor and Mrs Griggs Darling, it isn't the end of the world!
Barbara and Bernadette Don't say that!

The mothers go to their daughters and put their arms around them.

B. It wasn't the end of the world! It felt like it at the time.
Mrs Proctor and Mrs Griggs You've got your whole future in front of you!

In unison, the Dads, also in their end-of-the-play state, lower their papers and, simultaneously, speak directly to their individual daughters –

Dr Proctor and Mr Griggs What's up with your miserable face? [What's the matter with your greeting face?]

Mrs Proctor / Mrs Griggs Jim! / Frank!

The Dads relent from their initial – if unexplained – anger, soften.

Dr Proctor and Mr Griggs We won't say anything about this again, you hear me? Hush! (Wheesht!) You've got your whole future in front of you.

Lights change.

B. Thing is, we didn't think that meant much. Because next week we'd be dead. The whole world would have blown itself to smithereens. The headlines outside the newsagents said so. WAR INEVITABLE. Everybody was really scared, the grown-ups didn't talk about it, not in front of us kids, but we knew they knew it too. It was the end of the world. Tomorrow. The day after. Next week. Next week at the latest. This was the time of Cuba.

This photo must've been *before* that . . . Must have been that summer, end of term, and the Cuban missile crisis was, what, October? Well, look at the picture, Barbara and Bernadette are still joined at the hip. Friendship is still very much an item. This is the class of '62.

There's Miss Arthur. And Mr Shaw. Heartthrob. It doesn't take much. It doesn't take much, not with a class of fourteen-year-old girls, does it? And Old Cairncross, the headmaster, right slap in the middle between them. And there we are. Barbara and Bernadette, Berni and Barb. 'Barbara Proctor the Doctor's Daughter'. And Bernadette Griggs, 'one of those Griggs that Breed like Pigs'. Seven of a family, six boys, one girl.

Lights begin to fade down on the family tableaux.

Did you ever have a better friend than she was? Say it's a Saturday night. A *normal* Saturday night before

President Kennedy put the shits up the whole world
with his game of nuclear poker with the Russians.

*By the last line of the Chorus's speech the Girls are
together, downstage. It's Saturday night. They're alone,
bored and browsing through a pile of magazines.
Reading aloud sometimes.*

Chorus Have you one basic dress that can be dressed up
for almost any occasion?
Are both your stocking seams straight, this minute?
Have you at least one pair of plain black court shoes?
Bernadette What to do on that rare, that spare, night in?
Barbara Pamper yourself, of course!
Chorus To whiten grubby elbows, rub with a cut lemon
daily.
Bachelor Boys –
Bernadette Hollywood style . . .

*Barbara drops her boring magazine, grabs Bernadette's
and peruses.*

Chorus Rock Hudson finds home cooking great fun and
has a gang of his friends over once in a while to try out
his speciality. Barbecue spare ribs. And boy oh boy, do
they taste good.
Barbara John Wayne favours fish dishes.

Bernadette snatches the magazine from her.

Bernadette Dirk Bogarde prefers a rag out of veal.

Barbara snatches it back, looks.

Barbara Eh? *Ragout*, you! It's French, Bernadette.
Bernadette I know.
Chorus Tab Hunter is happy with a hamburger.
Bernadette I'm starving, Barbara!
Barbara Look! Taffy-haired Janet Leigh is the lovely wife
of actor Tony Curtis . . .

Bernadette Are they not divorced?

Barbara Maybe, it's an ancient magazine. Mum's had them for donkeys. She kids on she only gets them for the waiting room. Hah! (*She looks some more in the film magazine.*)

Bernadette Hollywood, eh?

Barbara Oh, I know . . .

Bernadette This place is a dump. See, when I'm seventeen, I'm going to dye my hair platinum, buy the highest stilettos I can find and emigrate to the USA.

Barbara dreams and yearns through the next list, each place more exotic and wonderful than the last.

Barbara Canada . . . New Zealand . . . Australia . . . Bernadette, you can go to Australia for ten quid.

Bernadette No, America. I'm dead serious, Barbara!

Barbara I know . . .

Bernadette I mean it! I've got an auntie in the States. New Jersey. Call this bloody Saturday night!

Barbara Here *is* a dump, isn't it?

Bernadette Here? I would not pee on it if it was on fire. They should drop the bomb on it any time. Do the world a favour.

Barbara Bernadette!

B. Don't say that, don't say it! In three days' time that'll be exactly what looks like happening.

The family tableaux fade back up, the Mums still ironing. Barbara and Bernadette separate and home in.

Go back . . . earlier that day . . . oh, fourteen years old and every Saturday it's the end of the world about *something*.

The two girls begin to wail. In unison, the Dads lower their papers, exasperated, and, simultaneously, directly at their individual daughters –

Dr Proctor and Mr Griggs What's up with your miserable face? [What's the matter with your greeting face?]
Barbara and Bernadette Nothing!
B. . . . Well, maybe you've picked out the pattern. Misses Petite Capri pants or toreadors . . . You'd place the pattern, you'd make yourself take the time to pin it, *patience*, patience and *pins*. You'd cut them out really, really carefully . . .
Chorus Suitable fabrics: seersucker, glazed cotton, knits, needlecord and piqué. Allow extra fabric to match large-scale prints.
B. Or your first fumbling experiments with last-thru 6 to 8 shampoo semi-permanent hair colour.
Chorus Chestnut Charm, Northern Lights, Golden Sequins . . .
B. Hint of a Tint. You'd spend hours in the chemist's poring over the colour chart. Disaster. And the biggest disaster of all? No effect. Total waste of money!

The Mums put down their irons, fold their arms, sigh in unison at their daughters and shake their heads.

Mrs Proctor and Mrs Griggs What a waste of money. You must have a lot more money than sense, my girl!
Mrs Griggs Bernadette! Don't you be leaving dirty marks all over my good towels!
Bernadette No, Mum.
Mrs Proctor Just watch, Barbara, you don't do any damage to my good Singer.
Barbara Right, Mum.
Mrs Griggs Don't you be long there in that bathroom. Your Dad's to get in there and get himself shifted.
Mrs Proctor And mind my shears!
Dr Proctor and Mr Griggs Hush! [Wheesht!]
Mrs Proctor Well, Jim, my good dressmaking shears and she uses them to cut her fringe.

Mrs Griggs Dyeing your hair at your age, what will the teachers say on Monday?

Barbara and Bernadette Mu-um . . .

Mrs Proctor What are you supposed to be making anyway?

Mrs Griggs What colour is it supposed to be going to turn out?

Barbara Toreador pants.

Bernadette Golden Sequins.

Mrs Proctor Jim, did you hear that!

Mrs Griggs What your dad will say I don't know!

Barbara and **Bernadette** Mu-um!

Mrs Proctor / Mrs Griggs Huh, *Tor*-eador pants! / Huh, Golden *Se*-quins!

Mrs Proctor Toreador pants, what are they when they are at home? With a BTM like yours? Frighten the French!

Mrs Griggs Make yourself cheap! Ends up bleached-looking your dad will tan your hide, my girl. What the hair-oil is Golden Sequins as a shade for hair?

Dr Proctor / Mr Griggs Nora! I am trying to do my – / Betty! I am trying to do my –

Mr Griggs bites back a two-beat expletive during Dr Proctor's line.

Dr Proctor – crossword!

Mr Griggs – coupon!

B. Sometimes I think the whole different backgrounds thing was grossly exaggerated, although much was made of it at the time. OK, different class, different attitudes, different standard of living, granted. Different sides of the track maybe, but I'd say they were far more alike than – well, certainly *much* more alike than they thought they were.

As if to prove how true this is, the families come out with their similar and overlapping little list of favourite homilies.

Dr Proctor and Mr Griggs Cut according to your cloth –
Dr and Mrs Proctor / Mr and Mrs Griggs A stitch in time
saves nine.
Dr and Mrs Proctor Many a mickle makes a muckle.
Mr and Mrs Griggs Watch your handbag.
Mrs Proctor People who complain of playing second
fiddle should be glad they're in the orchestra at all.
Dr and Mrs Proctor / Mr and Mrs Griggs You've got your
whole future in front of you!
Chorus You have got your whole future in front of you so
see you watch your handbag and stick in at the school.
Mrs Proctor and Mrs Griggs Saturday night, eh?
Barbara and Bernadette Big deal.

*There is an equal note of ever so slight sarcasm in each
of the Mum's next speeches.*

Mrs Proctor I suppose Berna*dette*'s coming round?
Mrs Griggs I suppose you'll be going round to *Bar*bara's?
Mrs Proctor / Mrs Griggs Or are you going there for a
change? / Or is she coming here for a change?
Mrs Proctor / Mrs Griggs Sometimes I wonder if she's a
home to go to! / Her mother will be wondering if you've
a home to go to!
Barbara and Bernadette Mu-um!
Mrs Griggs Bernadette, doll, just because you passed your
exam and qualified for the grammar school [high
school] there's no reason to treat your brothers like dirt
and turn up your nose at everybody else around here.
Mrs Proctor Barbara, pet, I know you and Bernadette
have been the best of pals since you were so high [yon
high], but now that you are at the big school have you
not made any other nice friends?
Mrs Griggs Don't you want to be pals with them?
Barbara and Bernadette Uh-huh, but my best pal's
Bernadette! / Uh-huh, but my best pal's Barbara!

The Mums shake their heads. Slowly lights fade on the
Mums and Dads.
    We're back with the girls alone with their pile of
magazines on a Saturday night.

Chorus To whiten grubby elbows, rub with a cut lemon
daily.
To lighten a sallow, winter-worn neck, make a bleaching
solution by mixing one tablespoon of twenty volume
peroxide to three drops ammonia.
Soak a wide strip of cotton wool, squeeze lightly and
wrap around the neck.
After twenty minutes, remove, splash skin with tepid
water and smear on a soothing cream.

Barbara I saw your big brother.

Bernadette Which big brother? My big big brother?

Barbara No, the nice-looking one, the next one.

Bernadette The apprentice? Nice-looking nothing!

Barbara Is he? With the bike. The butcher's boy.

Bernadette Butcher's boy? That's the third one and he is
ugly as a pig.

Barbara No he isn't.

Bernadette Is so.

Barbara Wish I had brothers . . .

Bernadette Pig ugly!

Barbara Wish I wasn't an only one . . .

Bernadette Wish I was an only one. My brothers are all
toerags. And this place is a dump.

Chorus Find your face shape here, then choose the style
famous London hairdresser Piers Von Spiers has created
specially for you . . .

Bernadette Barbara, would you say my face was round,
square, heart-shaped or oval.

Barbara Oval. Sort of a roundish oval. Or maybe it's
more of a squarish heart shape.

Bernadette I'm ugly.

Barbara Bernadette, you are not ugly. I'm ugly. I am pig ugly and Mr Shaw is getting married to Miss Arthur and I wish I was dead.

Lights change. The family tableaux begin to fade back up as B. speaks.

B. Don't say that, don't say it! Next week you'll wish you were back in this week, on a normal boring Saturday, making mountains out of molehills.

Back in their home spaces, Barbara, wailing, throws her botched sewing on the floor and, simultaneously, Bernadette, wailing just as loudly, flings down her towel in a temper.

Dr and Mrs Proctor / Mr and Mrs Griggs What's up with your face?

Barbara I cut the left leg-back out inside-out and squeegee.

Bernadette It's made no difference!

Barbara Supposed to be 'Simplicity'!

Mrs Proctor Nobody will notice.

Mrs Griggs Who's going to be looking at your hair anyway, you're only a little girl [wee lassie].

Dr Proctor and **Mr Griggs** I'll give you something to bloody cry for!

Mrs Proctor and **Mrs Griggs** Never mind, pet –

Mrs Proctor Bernadette's coming round, eh?

Mrs Griggs You're going round to Barbara's!

Barbara and **Bernadette** Where are you two going?

Mrs Proctor Just to the dinner dance at the golf club in aid of the Rotary.

Mrs Griggs Just round the pub [up the Miner's Welfare / the Club/the Legion, etc.] for a little [wee] drink.

Mrs Proctor and **Mrs Griggs** I didn't want to go . . . (*sigh*) It'll be no night out for me!

Mrs Proctor First it was where's his good black silk socks,

I says in your sock drawer beside your hankies, and I
suppose I'm to come and find your cummerbund and
your ready-tied bow-tie for you as per usual?

Mrs Griggs No night out for me, watching them pour
pints down their throats and arguing about outside lefts
and inside rights and bloody goalies. No –

Mrs Proctor and Mrs Griggs It'll be no night out for me
. . . (*sigh*) But it was your dad!

Mrs Proctor He'd bought the tickets.

Mrs Griggs Rose of Tralee came up first at the Dogs and
he promised Jack Thomson he'd buy him a pint.

Mrs Proctor and Mrs Griggs And it will be a night out, I
suppose.

Mrs Proctor A chance to give my silver shoes an outing –

Mrs Griggs Shift myself for a bit of a change [a wee change].

Mrs Proctor and Mrs Griggs And after all, it is Saturday
night!

*The Mums take off their aprons, smooth out their
dresses and twirl. The girls look on enviously.
As the Chorus speaks, the lights fade on the families and
the girls are alone on their Saturday night in.*

Chorus Single girls, how good a conversationalist are
you?
How bright will your visitors find the fireside chat this
winter?
Can you wash a woollen cardigan without shrinking it?
Do you know where the main stop cock is, for use when
there is a burst pipe?
Are you a stay-at-home with no wish to travel? (2 marks
for YES column A, or 2 marks for NO column C.)
Have you ever made (a) a dress, (b) a piece of basketry,
(c) a soufflé?

Barbara Did you not put that rinse through your hair?

Bernadette Uh-huh! Did you not finish your toreadors?

Barbara All right on Jackie Kennedy, but they'd never

have suited me anyway, an arse like mine.

Bernadette Can't you notice it a little bit [wee bit]?

Barbara It *is* nice and *shiny* . . .

Bernadette Look, I think it is just a rumour, about Mr Shaw and Miss Arthur. I hope it is only a rumour. For your sake.

Barbara Is it stuff just a rumour. He *is* getting married to her. Myra Simpson's big sister works beside Miss Arthur's cousin, who's a Saturday girl in Timothy White's the Chemist, and she's a bridesmaid. I only hope Arthur has the decency to wear a long white frock, piano legs like hers.

Bernadette She's got a nice face . . .

Barbara Up to a point. *Hellish* legs, you must admit it.

Bernadette I mean, I like her.

Barbara *I* like her. I *did* like her till she got her hooks in Mr Shaw.

Bernadette She's a good teacher.

Barbara He's a brilliant teacher.

Bernadette Barbara, you are only saying that because you fancy him.

Barbara I don't. You do.

Bernadette I don't. Not really. Barbara, I did do until I knew you did and then I decided you could because you've more chance with him than I do –

Barbara Bernadette, he's getting *married*.

Bernadette – and you're my friend. Barbara, we can't go around fancying the same people as each other any more, it just doesn't work out. So, he's getting married, that's nothing to us. Married, not married, that's not in our universe. But two best friends, Barbara, two best friends in love with the same man, disaster.

Barbara Can you do that, Bernadette? I don't think you can just decide about your feelings, that's not how it works.

Bernadette Oh yes it is, that's exactly how it works. Feelings is a decision.

Barbara I don't know . . . And anyway, I don't see how it matters if we both fancy the same person. I mean, we both fancied Richard Chamberlain last year, when everybody in the class went on to Ben Casey.

Bernadette That is totally different. Dr Kildare is a fictional character. But Mr Shaw is real.

Barbara Listen, Bernadette. I love him, and why I love him is he's such a brilliant teacher. With nice eyes.

Bernadette Whose pet are you.

Barbara I am not.

Bernadette You are. Teacher's pet. Mr Shaw's pet lamb [wee pet lamb] that's always the top of the class. *'I derived great pleasure from reading this essay. Eighteen out of twenty.' 'Barbara, would you read yours out loud?' 'I wish some of you would take a leaf out of Barbara Proctor's book.'* Barbara Proctor this, Barbara –

Barbara Look, drop it, will you, Berni? He's getting married.

Bernadette Are you sad?

Barbara remains silent, fuming with exasperation.

Tell you the truth, I'm sad he's getting married to Miss Arthur even though neither of the two of us has any chance anyway, even you that is his favourite, but . . . it's not the end of the world, you know.

Barbara Don't Tell Me What Is And Isn't The End Of The World. (*Pause.*) Read my fortune.

Bernadette I read your fortune on Wednesday. This is Saturday. You're supposed to give your future enough time to happen.

Barbara I didn't like that future. I want a different future.

Bernadette It's bad luck!

Barbara Get the book!

Chorus
> Your Fortune in the Cards.
> A Queen for a lady, A King for a gentleman,
> The suit according to his colouring – Hearts if very fair,
> Diamonds if fairish,
> Clubs if rather dark, Spades if very dark,
> Will represent the person with whom you are, or are
> destined to be,
> In love.

The cards are spread out before Barbara, who looks at them horrified, while Bernadette consults the 'luck book'.

Bernadette Five of Clubs, a quarrel with a friend or at work. That's school, we don't go to work. A quarrel with a friend or at school. Seven of Spades, injustice, Nine . . . danger or risk. Nine of diamonds, news good or bad depending on the cards next to it. The Ace of Spades, reversed . . .

B. Two days after Bernadette wished the bomb would fall on this dump and Barbara wished she was dead and they brought bad luck on themselves tempting fate by asking for a different fortune too soon, it really began to look as if they were about to get their wishes.

Lights come up again on the ironing boards and home sets, the Mums still ironing and the Dads still with their papers.

On Monday night after *The Archers* they announced on the radio that President Kennedy will address the American nation at midnight our time. On a matter of the Greatest National Urgency.

The Dads put down their newspapers, faces worried, listening. The Mums stop and upend the irons on their boards.

Mrs Proctor and Mrs Griggs Uh-oh! (*They fold their arms and bite their lips.*)

B. He told how Russian missile bases were being built on the island of Cuba, just ninety miles off the Florida coast, easy striking distance from American soil.

Chorus . . . The purpose of these bases can be none other than to provide a nuclear strike capability against the West . . .

B. The United States were united in their hatred of Cuba, Communism, a revolution and a man called Castro. And very, very frightened by his alliance with Russia.

Chorus . . . capable of striking Washington DC, the Panama Canal, Cape Canaveral . . .

B. Kennedy demanded the 'withdrawal of Soviet offensive missiles from Cuba' and imposed a 'naval quarantine' – that was the word he used –

Chorus – a quarantine on all ships carrying weapons to Cuba.

B. Then it got to the bit when you knew it was really scary.

Chorus US strategic forces are on full alert. Any missile launched from Cuba will be regarded as a Soviet missile and will be met by a full retaliatory response.

Dr Proctor and Mr Griggs That sounds like that'll be the balloon about to go up!

Barbara and Bernadette What balloon?

Dr Proctor and Mr Griggs Never mind!

Mrs Proctor Hush, Jim [Wheesht, Jim], in front of Barbara.

Mrs Griggs Hush, Frank [Wheesht, Frank], you'll have all the kids [bairns/weans] terrified out of their wits!

B. You knew there was going to be a war, and they knew there was going to be a war, and all the bad dreams you'd ever had about the atom bomb and the four-minute warning and the noise of the sirens when they tested them – it was all coming true at last.

Dr Proctor That Khrushchev! We should've sorted out the Russians at the end of the last war.

Mr Griggs That bloody Kennedy, he's going to get us all killed trying to get himself re-elected president.

B. Next morning the newspaper headlines were all big black letters and the words CRISIS and CUBA. Yet everything, everything on the surface, was absolutely normal and you just went to school as usual. On the third day, the scariest day so far, of the Cuba Crisis, we went to Miss Arthur for Modern Studies.

The parents speak out from a different, earlier, time now, the time at the beginning of term when they first heard of the new subject. They are laughing.

Mrs Proctor Jim!

Mrs Griggs Frank!

Mrs Proctor and Mrs Griggs Do you hear that?

Dr Proctor 'Modern Studies', what's that when it's at home?

Barbara and Bernadette It's a mixture of Geography, History, Economics –

Mr Griggs At least it sounds like something useful and not that [yon] bloody Latin and Greek dead languages carry-on!

Mrs Proctor and Mrs Griggs Economics!

Mrs Griggs You'd know all about economics if you tried to keep you lot in school shoes on what they pay your father!

Barbara and Bernadette It's a mixture of Geography, History, Economics and Current Affairs.

Mrs Proctor speaks with mock humility but an amused scorn for such a ridiculous new-fangled non-subject.

Mrs Proctor Oh well, what did the poor child know!

Lights change, the parents fade, all the girls in the Chorus become a classroom seated in pairs, Barbara and Bernadette in the middle. Miss Arthur is writing a word on a central, invisible 'fourth wall' blackboard. She turns to the class.

Miss Arthur Block-ade. What does the word 'blockade' mean? (*She looks about the class before picking at random.*) Sandra?
Sandra Miss, it's where the navy stops ships landing their cargo at an enemy port.
Miss Arthur Exactly. A blockade is a naval siege. Such as President Kennedy is currently conducting on Cuba. But he didn't actually use the word 'blockade' in his speech. Any idea why? (*Pause.*) No? Nobody? Well, he used another word instead? Anybody? He used the word 'quarantine'. What does the word 'quarantine' mean? I mean normally. Marianne? No?

Marianne shakes her head. Linda volunteers.

Linda In a hospital, Miss.
Miss Arthur *What* 'in a hospital'? Yes?
Barbara Miss, it's where you isolate somebody that's full of germs to stop them infecting anybody else.
Miss Arthur Very good. Yes. So it's an interesting use of the word in this case, isn't it?
Maureen Miss, it means America wants to stop Cuba from getting infected with Communism.
Eleanor Bernadette Griggs's dad's a Communist.
Bernadette He is not!
Beth Bernadette Griggs's dad says there is going to be a war.
Miss Arthur Well, I fervently hope not, but Bernadette's dad could be right . . .
Barbara Miss, there isn't going to be a world war, is there?

Sandra and Maureen Will there be a war?

Bernadette Why do we still have to come to school? Why do we have to do hockey when there is going to be a war?

Linda, Jean-Ann, Susan and Marianne Miss, is there going to be World War Three?

Miss Arthur I *hope* not. Back to this language though.

Barbara Mr Shaw said there wasn't going to be a war.

Miss Arthur skates easily and neutrally over the personal nature of Mr Shaw's name being mentioned in her classroom.

Miss Arthur I very much hope he is right.

Bernadette pushes Barbara's taboo-breaking further, and more consciously than her friend.

Bernadette *Mr Shaw* said that the atom bomb has kept the peace since the end of the last war.

Miss Arthur Well, that's a point of view . . .

Linda Miss, are you in CND?

Jean-Ann Miss, is it true that you're a Ban the Bomber?

Maureen Miss, you look like a Ban the Bomber in your duffle-coat!

Susan Miss, are you engaged to Mr Shaw?

Miss Arthur, beleaguered, just answers nothing and shouts to regain control.

Miss Arthur NOW, THE AMERICAN BLOCKADE OF CUBA! Why didn't Kennedy use the word?

Bernadette Call a spade a spade.

Miss Arthur Exactly. Any ideas? Well, it was probably a matter of international law. Mr Gaitskell – Mr Gaitskell? Anybody?

Marianne The Leader of the Opposition.

Miss Arthur Right! Mr Gaitskell has raised the question of the legality of the American action in blockading

Cuba. A blockade is an act of war. Does one country have the right – in time of peace – to blockade another country by posting its navy in international waters? Also Gaitskell, and others – not the Prime Minister, not Macmillan, or at least not publicly, but many on the left – expressed their grave concern at the lack of consultation between the USA and its NATO partners. NATO, Jean-Ann Simpson?

Jean-Ann North Atlantic . . . North Atlantic . . .

Pamela North Atlantic Treaty Organization.

Miss Arthur Good, Pamela . . .

Bernadette My dad says Kennedy is crazy and he could kill us all trying to get re-elected.

Beth Everybody knows it's Khrushchev that's off his nut.

Eleanor He is! He's crazy. He's a Communist.

Pamela He wears funny suits.

Miss Arthur Is that important?

Eleanor Mrs Khrushchev wears big stupid bundles of lumpy fur coats and she looks worse than somebody out of the Women's Institute [Women's Guild].

Maureen Russian women have to drive tractors!

Pamela Mrs Kennedy looks like someone out of a woman's magazine. Jackie Kennedy looks like a million dollars.

Beth Khrushchev is a maniac.

Bernadette You just believe all the propaganda.

Beth It's the Communists that do propaganda.

Miss Arthur Ah, now we see – calm down, Beth, ssh! Bernadette – 'propaganda' is lies spread by the other side. 'Truth' is *our* side's view of the matter.

Bernadette 'Truth is beauty and beauty truth.' That's what Mr Shaw says.

Miss Arthur Good for him . . .

Barbara That's back-to-front, you. Anyway, it's John Keats!

Miss Arthur Good for him, but we were discussing the

current situation. Possible ways out. Of this dangerous situation. The United States could trade *their* bases in Turkey, which are after all just as close to the USSR as these ones the Russians want to build on Cuba are to American soil.

Sandra That's totally different!

Miss Arthur How is it totally different, Sandra?

Sandra It is! My dad says Churchill should've finished off the Russians at the end of the last war. He says the Russkies are worse than the Germans any day. Communism's worse than the Nazis.

Susan So does mine. He says the Yanks should bomb the Cuban bases and invade straight away, show Khrushchev who is the boss.

Miss Arthur Well, let's hope no one takes that course in the present incendiary situation . . .

Maureen My dad says what this country needs is another war to get this country on its feet.

Bernadette Then your dad's a maniac like President Kennedy.

Miss Arthur Now, now . . .

Bernadette Well, Bertrand Russell sent him a telegram telling him so!

Barbara So he did.

Barbara and Bernadette stand up and speak out in choric fashion as everyone else freezes, amazed.

Barbara and Bernadette 'Your action desperate. Stop. No conceivable justification. Stop. We will not have mass murder. Stop. End this madness. Stop.'

B. It got worse and worse, though. The Russian forces were on full alert. Khrushchev *was* crazy, we all knew that. He wore lumpy suits and Cossack hats and was bald and crazy like an angry baby. At the UN he took off his shoe and banged it on the table and shouted like a furious tyrannical baby determined to get his own way

23

or bring the whole house down on everybody's head.

Lights change. The Chorus are singing the last verse of the hymn at school assembly.

Chorus
Hobgoblin nor foul fiend
  Can daunt his spirit;
He knows he at the end
  Shall life inherit
Then fancies fly away;
  He'll fear not what men say;
He'll labour night and day
  To be a pilgrim.

Mr Cairncross Let us pray. O Lord, Bless this school, and make all of us loyal, obedient and useful citizens in this our school community.
Lord, today in our school assembly, we pray for our country and the world. Bless our leaders in this time of international tension. God bless Mr Macmillan and President Kennedy. They know the course they have embarked on is right and just, and we pray that you will grant them courage to keep to this right course and to have the strength to prevail against those dishonourable peacemongers who would have them compromise with the forces of evil. We thank God for the strength of our leaders in the face of intolerable provocation.
We know that it is only when faced with our courage that our enemies will see the error of their ways.

Lights change. Barbara and Bernadette move out of that central position in the Chorus downstage to where they are talking alone together, probably in the same space as their 'Saturday night' scene.

Bernadette Jeez, that Cairncross is as mad as the rest of them, Barbara. Bloody headmasters . . .
Barbara I know. It's getting worse. There are all these

Russian ships stopped dead in the water just in front of
the US Navy. If any of these lunatics fire, Bernadette . . .

Bernadette I know. Madmen. I think it's men that's mad.

Barbara You mean 'mankind'?

Bernadette No, men. Women wouldn't play at cowboys
like this.

Barbara Women don't get the chance. Women don't get to
be the president of the United States. Women don't get
to be the prime minister.

Bernadette I'll tell you whose side I'm on.

Barbara Whose?

Bernadette Cuba's.

Barbara Cuba. But my dad says Cuba's just a prawn.

Bernadette A what?

Barbara I mean a pawn, Berni, you know what I mean. I
mean just a toy. In Khrushchev's game.

Bernadette Exactly. That's why I'm on Cuba's side.

*Lights change. Instead of Miss Arthur, Mr Shaw stands
in front of the class. Bernadette and Barbara move back
to their central places in the classroom.*

Mr Shaw All right, 3A! Put away your *Merchant of
Venice*s. We'll stop there, end of Act Two, till next week.

*Barbara and Bernadette are talking in asides to each
other.*

Barbara If there is a next week.

Mr Shaw Take out your *Approach to Poetry*s. We've got
twenty minutes or so left and we can continue on the
Romantics. I'd like to get to Wordsworth by Christmas.

Bernadette Imagine this might be the final Double English
we ever get and we've got to waste it on Poetry.

Mr Shaw Barbara Proctor and Bernadette Griggs, are you
two chatting? If you've got something to say, share it
with us all, please.

Bernadette Even on Death Row, eh, the guys get to pick

what they want for their last breakfast, don't they?

Mr Shaw Bernadette Griggs, stand up! Repeat what you just said!

Bernadette is embarrassed and apologetic.

Bernadette I . . . just said . . . 'On Death Row the condemned men get their favourite meal the day of their execution,' Sir.

Mr Shaw Fascinating! I won't ask from what lurid film on ITV you gleaned this riveting information. Nor will I ask you to explain its dubious relevance to the topic on hand. Which is the Romantic Poetry of the early nineteenth century. John Keats, Bernadette Griggs?

Bernadette A . . . a Romantic poet, Sir.

Mr Shaw OK, sit down, Bernadette. And no more chattering!

Bernadette No, Sir.

Mr Shaw A Romantic poet. Anything else? Anybody . . .

Eleanor He died, Sir.

Mr Shaw He died, Eleanor, like we all will someday. But yes, John Keats died very young, at the age of twenty-three, of consumption. But not before writing some of the finest, most beautiful, sensuous poems in the English language. (*Mr Shaw turns to an imaginary blackboard out front and 'writes' on it in invisible schoolmaster's copperplate.*) 'Beauty is truth, truth beauty.' John Keats, 'Ode on a Grecian Urn'. Write it down.

Bernadette Sir, we did last week.

Mr Shaw All right, Bernadette! Write it down again then. Beauty is truth, truth beauty. Think about that. (*Pause.*) Turn to page thirty-eight. Marianne, you start, a verse each. 'La Belle Dame sans Merci'. Translation, please.

No one volunteers until Bernadette, trying to get back in his good books, tentatively sticks her hand up.

All right, Bernadette . . .

Bernadette 'The Beautiful Ungrateful Woman'.
Mr Shaw How do you make that out? Oh, I see . . .
  Literally! . . . Pamela!
Pamela 'The . . . Beautiful Woman without Thanks'?
Mr Shaw Yes, only here I think it means something much
  closer to the English 'mercy'. First verse, Marianne!

*Mr Shaw picks at random by pointing to them, each
member of the Chorus, before each verse. Different
amounts of volume and commitment but somehow the
poem rings out clear.*

Marianne
  O what can ail thee, knight-at-arms,
    Alone and palely loitering?
  The sedge is wither'd from the lake,
    And no birds sing.
Eleanor
  O what can ail thee, knight-at-arms,
    So haggard and so woe-begone?
  The squirrel's granary is full,
    And the harvest's done.
Pamela
  I see a lily on thy brow
    With anguish moist and fever dew,
  And on they cheeks a fading rose
    Fast withereth too.
Maureen
  I met a lady in the meads,
    Full beautiful – a faery's child,
  Her hair was long, her foot was light,
    And her eyes were wild.
Susan
  I made a garland for her head,
    And bracelets too, and fragrant zone,
  She look'd at me as she did love,
    And made sweet moan.

Linda
  I set her on my pacing steed,
    And nothing else saw all day long,
  For sidelong would she bend, and sing
    A faery's song.

Beth
  She found me roots of relish sweet,
    And honey wild, and manna dew,
  And sure in language strange she said –
    'I love thee true!'

Jean-Ann
  She took me to her elfin grot,
    And there she gazed and sigh'd full sore,
  And there I shut her wild, wild eyes
    With kisses four.

Sandra
  And there she lullèd me asleep
    And there I dream'd – ah! woe betide!
  The latest dream I ever dream'd
    On the cold hill's side.

Bernadette
  I saw pale kings and princes too,
    Pale warriors, death-pale were they all;
  They cried – 'La Belle Dame sans Merci
    Hath thee in thrall!'

*Barbara, deeply affected both by the poem and the
nuclear threat, which seem to her suddenly somehow
powerfully connected, struggles to get her verse out.*

Barbara
  I saw their . . . starved lips in the gloam,
    With . . . with horrid warning gapèd wide,
  And I a– And I awoke . . .

*Barbara breaks down completely. Mr Shaw is
embarrassed, increasingly disconcerted as he fails to calm*

her, completely out of his depth. He feels responsible,
though he would be hard pressed to explain why.

Mr Shaw Barbara, Barbara, pet, what's the matter? Do
you want to go for a drink of water?

Barbara No. No, I don't . . .

Mr Shaw Bernadette, take Barbara for a drink of water,
wash your face, huh? It's OK.

Barbara It's not!

Mr Shaw Take her to see Miss Houselander, tell her she's
not feeling well.

Barbara I don't want to! I don't want to!

Mr Shaw What's wrong?

Barbara I'm frightened. (*She finds an almost defiantly*
clear voice to admit what, despite their questions in Miss
Arthur's class, nobody's been actually admitting in so
many words.) I'm frightened there's going to be a war.

Mr Shaw Ah . . . (*All his natural kindness comes out and*
he drops all that grammar school teacher's pomposity.)
Listen, listen, don't cry. Don't worry. I don't think –
really – we have anything to worry about. How many of
you have been worrying themselves about the . . .
international situation?

At first stragglingly slowly, following Barbara's defiant
admission, gradually all the hands go up. He is very
moved.

Mr Shaw Well, the situation is not good, I wouldn't
pretend otherwise, but honestly –

Barbara Sir, I read a book about Hiroshima. The atom
bombs they dropped at the end of the war . . . The
people were turned to ashes. They were as thin as
photographs, burned on to the buildings, like printed
shadows on the brick and stone. And in Nagasaki a
man saw a burning horse in the heart of the city and its
foal ran by its side and there was no skin or flesh on it,

just bare sinews and muscles, and its eyes peeled and its mouth screaming.

Mr Shaw Good God, what are your parents thinking about letting you read a book like that, sensitive girl like you?

Linda Is there really going to be a war, Sir?

Mr Shaw Now, I really think, honestly, that this is a game the world leaders are playing. They know exactly how far to go. They can take it right to the brink, then pull back. They don't want a war either. That's the last thing they want! A nuclear war is one nobody can win and they know that. Nuclear weapons have probably saved world peace ever since the end of World War Two. Because it's a balance. No one could win. They won't do it . . . Are you listening to me? I'm not frightened, and I assure you I am one of the world's great cowards . . . Dry your eyes. Come on, Barbara. Are you all right?

Barbara Yes, Sir.

Mr Shaw Good. Are you feeling better?

An eventual nod and a sniff.

Good. Well enough to read?

Another nod.

Excellent. Now will you read for us till the end of the poem?

Barbara breathes deep and reads clearly.

Barbara
I saw their starved lips in the gloam,
  With horrid warning gapèd wide,
And I awoke and found me here,
  On the cold hill's side.

And this is why I sojourn here,

30

    Alone and palely loitering,
  Though the sedge is wither'd from the lake,
    And no birds sing.

Lights snap change and back up on B. Alone.

B. In October 1962, at the height of the Cuba Crisis, we
  hid, after the Thursday After-school Chess Club, in the
  toilets, where the cleaners had already been, and waited
  till the school emptied.

*Lights up on Bernadette and Barbara. They stand in
front of a door which has on it, in gold letters,*
HEADMASTER. MR J. K. CAIRNCROSS, M.A. *They are
shaking up aerosol cans with that satisfying rattle.*

Barbara Have you ever stolen anything before?
Bernadette No . . .
Barbara Me neither.
Bernadette Not even when you were little [wee], sweets
  out of the newsagent's?
Barbara No.
Bernadette My big big brother when he was little
  [wee]stole two Mars Bars and the policeman brought
  him home. By the ear. My father kicked his arse for him
  and it put us all off.
Barbara I enjoyed it.
Bernadette So did I.
Barbara Woolworths was the easiest, but these car paints
  out of Halfords are the best.
Bernadette Brilliant colour!
Barbara Were you scared?
Bernadette No.
Barbara Where did you say you were?
Bernadette I said I was going to yours to do my
  homework. What did you say?
Barbara I said I was going to yours.
Bernadette Barbara, do you promise?

31

Barbara Yes.

Bernadette Blood sisters?

Barbara Blood sisters till the end of the world, Amen.

*Bernadette cuts her thumb with a penknife, wincing.
Barbara takes it, shuts her eyes, does the same. They
press their hands together and watch one loud drop
down to the floor. Barbara sucks her thumb, shakes the
aerosol up hard, and she is the one to fiercely aerosol,
large messy and scarlet across the headmaster's door,
the word* CUBA. *They stand back and look, then
Bernadette shakes again and this time sprays* CUBA
LIBRE.

Bernadette Cu-ba Li-bre.

Barbara What's that?

Bernadette Free Cuba! I wish Kennedy and Khrushchev
would leave it alone and let them have their revolution
and their Fidel Castro and his Havana cigars.

Barbara Ssh!

They are both whispering.

Bernadette What?

Barbara There is somebody coming. There is!

Bernadette Hide!

Barbara Where?

*They flatten themselves against the (imaginary) wall
either side of the door, breathing hard. They are afraid.
Looking in each other's eyes, a solemn and
preoccupied Mr Shaw and Miss Arthur, he with his arm
around her, come round the corner. Stop dead.*

Mr Shaw What the hell is going on?

Lights change. Back up on B. alone.

B. Looking back now, I suppose Mr Shaw and Miss
Arthur had stayed late at school to make love. After all,

Mr Shaw lived with his widowed mother in a bungalow down Orchard Drive, everybody knew that. Miss Arthur – well, no doubt she had a similar impossible domestic parental situation.

Mr Shaw, as head of department, had a walk-in book cupboard with an armchair and cups and an electric kettle. I had seen all this when I was sent once to collect a set of *Far from the Madding Crowd*s. No doubt he had a tartan picnic rug too, and an old one-bar electric fire. I have made happy love myself in far more uncomfortable situations.

And it's true what they say about sex and death, isn't it? We were very close to death that week.

Anyway, I could tell they felt caught out themselves, catching us.

The girls sit side by side, with Mr Shaw standing over. Miss Arthur tugs at his arm, murmurs. But he doesn't waver.

Miss Arthur Stewart, just let them go . . . Think about it! Better off – from everybody's point of view – We weren't here, we saw nothing.

Mr Shaw What on earth is the meaning of this? Are you crazy? How were you going to get out of the school anyway? You were locked in!

Bernadette I don't know . . .

Mr Shaw You don't know! What the – has the whole world gone mad?

Miss Arthur I think that's rather the point, Stewart.

B. She dragged him away to one side. We just sat there. But we could hear every word they were saying nevertheless.

Miss Arthur They are really, really upset.

Mr Shaw They are upset! Hell, Joyce, we are all upset. I'd never have believed this. My best – (*here he catches himself before saying 'best pupil' and includes Bernadette*) *two* of my very best pupils –

Miss Arthur They won't do it again, Stew . . .

Mr Shaw By God they won't. Joyce, we have to report this to Cairncross first thing in the morning and God knows –

Miss Arthur Give me your keys, Stewart. (*She holds out her hand.*)

Mr Shaw What?

Miss Arthur Give me the car keys.

Mr Shaw Joyce?

Miss Arthur I'll drive them home. They're upset. Go to the Royal Oak. I'll meet you in the Royal Oak later.

He hands over the car keys. Lights change. Up on B. Alone.

B. She drove us home. She didn't say anything. She didn't come in and say anything to our parents, she even let each of us off at the end of our roads so we wouldn't be seen getting out of a car and have to answer any awkward questions. All she said to both of us was she would see us in the morning, we must come to school as usual, and that everything would be all right.

Lights change. Chorus together as a class again. Mr Prentiss's (or Miss Prentiss's) Latin class. Prentiss is the classic Classics teacher who can't keep order, old and deaf to all conversations, carries on regardless in a world of his or her own, therefore it is easy for Bernadette and Barbara to talk openly to each other with little sense of the 'aside'.

Prentiss '*Carpite nunc, tauri*' – '*tauri*'? Maureen Miller?

Maureen Bulls, Sir [Miss].

Bernadette She said it would be OK. Miss Arthur is magnificent.

Prentiss '*Carpite nunc, tauri, de septum montibus herbas dum licet*' – 'Seize while you may, O bulls, the grass of the seven hills.'

Barbara They'll tell. They're bound to.

Prentiss Seven hills, Susan Lockwood?

Barbara It doesn't matter. We'll be dead next week, like Bertrand Russell says.

Susan Seven hills of Rome, Sir [Miss]?

Bernadette The Russian ships have changed course. It said it on the news this morning.

Prentiss Seven hills of Rome, precisely. For, as we see, '*Hic magnae iam locus urbis erit.*'

Bernadette Glimmer of hope, that's what it said.

Prentiss Sandra? No? Jean-Ann?

Barbara I think there is no hope and there is no hope they won't report us.

Jean-Ann 'Here was the place of a great city' –

Prentiss '*Erit*', Jean-Ann, '*erit*'!

Barbara They're *teachers*.

Prentiss Future tense!

Bernadette I think we're safe.

Prentiss Future tense! 'Here *shall* be the site of a great city.' '*Roma, tuum nomen*' . . . 'Rome, your name' . . .

Bernadette Look at it this way, Barbara, what were they doing in the school together so late?

Prentiss '*Militat omnis amans et habet sua castra Cupido.*' 'Lovers are soldiers all, in Cupid's' – literally 'in Cupid's *camp*' . . . 'in Cupid's private army.'

Bernadette Imagine, Barbara, if the bomb fell and you'd still never even done it?

Prentiss 'Lovers are soldiers all in Cupid's private army.' Ovid.

A Girl enters and advances towards Prentiss's desk.

Ovid, the great Latin poet. Ah, a messenger approaches!

Messenger Girl Please, Mr Prentiss [Miss Prentiss], Mr Cairncross wants to see Bernadette Griggs and Barbara Proctor right away.

*Prentiss is jocular, not believing two model pupils can
be guilty of anything serious.*

Prentiss Right away! What have you two been up to, eh?
Barbara Proctor, Bernadette Griggs, to the headmaster's
office.

*They stand up and, clenching themselves, follow the
Messenger out of the room space as Prentiss continues.*

'. . . *ut eat sacer agnus ad aras.*' 'See the sacred lamb
advances to the shining altar.'

*Lights change, focus on B. and, as she speaks, the
classroom scene dissolves and the free-standing door, the
graffiti-ed door, is pushed on by two cleaners with mops
and pails. This time it is placed backstage and round the
other way so that downstage becomes inside Cairncross's
office. The cleaners open the door and get to work.*

B. Mr Shaw was inside with Cairncross. Behind closed
doors – well, they *would* have been closed, but two
cleaners were attacking our lovely graffiti with soap,
water and strippers, so they stood wide to the world.
And we could hear every word.

*Lights change. Barbara and Bernadette walk grimly
together towards the office door. Cairncross, in the
office with Shaw. Looks upstage and sees them. He
walks upstage and calls through the door to them.*

Mr Cairncross Sit down. You two sit down there until I
am ready to deal with you.

*The two chairs he indicates are side on, facing inwards,
in either near corner, just along the wall from the door
of what would be the outer hall of his office. Thus
Barbara and Bernadette are symmetrically placed facing
each other as they overhear Cairncross and Shaw.
Barbara looks at the floor. Bernadette often responds to*

*what she hears by looking at the friend who won't meet
her eye.*

Mr Shaw Mr Cairncross, I really think this has been a
case of one weak pupil being led astray by a stronger
and far more wicked nature. Barbara Proctor is a very
sensitive girl, a very gifted pupil. I don't think I've had a
better in all the years I've been teaching.

Mr Cairncross The doctor's daughter? Jim Proctor's
daughter? I know him well. Play golf with him. Her
mother is a distinguished former pupil of this school,
you know. Captain of the School, 1938–9. I know that
because it was the year after I pipped Jim Proctor to the
post for Dux of the Boys' Grammar [Boys' High]. Used
to dance with her at the tennis club dances when I was
home on leave during the war. Who's the other girl?

Mr Shaw Bernadette Griggs.

Mr Cairncross Griggs? I don't know any Griggses . . .

*Miss Arthur approaches the girls and the headmaster's
office.*

B. Miss Arthur came along then. She went white when she
saw us. She came and stood beside us. She took us each
by the hand.

*Miss Arthur takes Bernadette by the hand from her
chair and leads her to the other side of the door and
Barbara's place, where their threesome can clearly be
seen. She takes Barbara's hand and she stands up too.
Miss Arthur holds each girl by one hand, which she
squeezes, steeling herself too.*

Miss Arthur Courage . . .

Cairncross goes to the door.

Mr Cairncross Come in, you two. I told you to sit there!
Miss Arthur! Don't you have a class . . .

Miss Arthur still holds both girls by the hand. They enter the study.

Miss Arthur Not right now, Mr Cairncross. I've got a free lesson.

Mr Cairncross Don't you have some marking . . .

Miss Arthur Don't punish these girls!

Mr Cairncross Miss Arthur!

Miss Arthur I warned you, Stewart, and I meant it. Here's your ring.

She takes it off and holds it out to him. He cringes, mortified.

Mr Shaw Joyce, for goodness' sake, this is neither the time nor the place . . .

Miss Arthur Take it! Or I'll throw it on the floor. (*Pause.*) Take it!

Mr Shaw takes the ring and pockets it.

Mr Cairncross Miss Arthur, leave us please. I have something to discuss with you later. I have had complaints, complaints from several parents about you frightening the girls, frightening the girls and . . . and . . . political indoctrination!

Miss Arthur I resign. Headmaster, I wish to give in my notice.

His jaw opens and shuts. He is amazed. Miss Arthur walks out, head held high. Cairncross turns on the girls. Their heads are down. They are quaking, silent.

Mr Cairncross Now what do you two have to say for yourselves?

Silence.

Nothing?

Silence.

Nothing! What is the meaning of this wanton
   destructiveness?

*Bernadette's head goes up and she speaks out loud and
clear.*

Bernadette Cuba. Cuba Libre.
Mr Cairncross What is this nonsense?
Bernadette I wrote it on the wall. Kennedy is mad.
   Kennedy is mad and Khrushchev is mad. I am a beldam,
   I am a beldam sans merci. Cuba Libre!
Mr Cairncross Keep quiet! Barbara Proctor, what do you
   have to say for yourself?

Silence.

I'm waiting.

Silence.

Come on!

Silence. It holds. Barbara stares at the floor.
   *Bernadette looks at Barbara astonished, willing her to
speak. Gives up. Makes the decision to save Barbara's
skin if that's what she wants. Maybe there is scorn in
such a decision, maybe it is one last attempt to remind
her of her blood-sister promise, but anyway she speaks
out to save her friend.*

Bernadette It was my idea. Basically, it was my idea and
   Barbara just went along with me.
Mr Cairncross Well? Well? What do *you* have to say?

*Barbara still stares at the floor. Silence. B. speaks out,
using loud and clear for the first time the word 'I' –
which she gives full emphasis and value to – owning up
to which role she played in this early personal drama,
revealing her identity.*

B. I said nothing. All I had to say was that it wasn't true.

Though it was, sort of . . . Indeed, it *was* Bernadette's idea to become CUBA, the two-girl gang, but I had been wild to be a part of it. I stole the red car paint, I made the first mark on Cairncross's door.

Lights slowly come up on the Mums ironing. The Dads in their chairs. The same domestic spaces as before.

And I was 'severely disciplined'. My parents were called in, I was stripped of my class vice-captain's badge, banned from any school outings, denied all privileges for the rest of the term.
While Bernadette was expelled.

Barbara and Bernadette, in a reprise of their first approach to their families, heads down in shame, go slowly to their Mums, who hold back for one beat, then embrace them. The girls weep silently in their mothers' arms.

Mrs Proctor Ssh, ssh, darling, it isn't the end of the world!

Dr Proctor puts his newspaper up in front of his face.

Mrs Griggs Never mind, darlin', it's not the end of the world.

*Mr Griggs put his newspaper up in front of his face.
   And both these symmetrical family tableaux, mothers with arms still round daughters, hold till the end of the play.*

B. It wasn't. Cuba fizzled out. Touch and go, everybody said that. We'd been hours away from Armageddon. If Khrushchev hadn't withdrawn on Sunday . . . But they did, and the crisis was over, in exchange for a promise that America would never again invade Cuba and, unofficially, for some of those American bases in Turkey. The important thing was that nobody was to lose face. In America it was to be victory for Kennedy, and in

Russia victory for Khrushchev.
Bernadette and I were never friends again. When we were
forced to pass each other in the street she would look
through me and I would just look away. Usually she
would be with some other friends of hers, from the rough
school.
But, to this day, any time there is anything on TV about
Kennedy . . . whether it is about him and Marilyn
Monroe, or another theory about who it actually was
that pulled the trigger that fired the fatal shot that killed
the President on the motorcade in Dallas, every time, I
think of Cuba.
And Bernadette. I think of her as 'La Belle Dame sans
Merci' . . .

*The Chorus as a photograph, as at the beginning of the
play.*

Chorus
I met a lady in the meads,
    Full beautiful – a faery's child,
Her hair was long, her foot was light,
    And her eyes were wild.

DOG HOUSE

Gina Moxley

Characters

Ger, fourteen
Debs, fourteen, Ger's best friend
Mossie, sixteen, Ger's boyfriend
Jimmy, sixteen, a neighbour
Marian, fourteen, a neighbour
Connie, eighteen, father of Ger's sister Dee's baby
Barry, seventeen, a neighbour
Finn, twenty-two, Ger's brother
Aideen, twenty-one, Finn's wife
The Martin family a.k.a. **The Flying Saucers:**
Val, sixteen
Dessie, fifteen
Pats, fourteen
Bridget, twelve

The play is set in a cul-de-sac called Lime Lawn, the suburbs of Cork city.

SCENE ONE

*Ger is standing at the gate to her house at the end of the
cul-de-sac chatting to her best pal, Debs. Both are
dressed in jeans and sloppy jumpers. Debs is sitting on
her bike.*

Debs Eight pounds twelve ounces. I don't believe you.
Gawd, that's massive. It's gas, isn't it, so small going in
and so big coming out.

Ger Don't let Connie hear you saying that.

Debs The idea of it.

Ger I know. You'd eat him without salt though, he's
absolutely gorgeous.

Debs Yeah, but Ger, eight pound twelve ounces. That's
not a baby at all, that's a teenager practically. She must
be in flitters, is she?

Ger Shreds, girl. Something like sixteen stitches.

Debs Sixteen.

Ger And then they were worried that she might get
toxaemia on top of everything else.

Debs What's that when it's out?

Ger Something to do with blood poisoning, or is it blood
pressure? I'm not sure. They thought she might have to
have a section, but in the end she was grand.

Debs That's good, no scar at least. She'll still be able to
wear a bikini.

Ger Eventually, when she gets her figure back like. I'd say
that's the least of her worries, Debs.

Debs Yeah. You'll have the barbed wire up for Mossie
now. God, I wouldn't be able for it, would you?

They both shake their heads.

45

Ger (*laughing*) You'd want to have seen the state of
Connie, pacing up and down like a hen on stubble.
Then when the doctors came out and told him that he
was a father and it was a boy, he did a gawk in the
corridor. A big vom. I swear. All pints, of course.

Debs The place must've been reeking of stale stout. Poor
old Connie. I can just see him.

Ger The nuns weren't a bit happy with him being in there
in the first place like, but that really put the kibosh on it.
You know what they're like. The place is immaculate.

Debs Old wagons.

Ger Mercy is right. Whoever thought up that name for
them had some sense of humour, that's for sure.

Debs I know. Savages'd be nearer the mark. I'm sure he
didn't take a tack of notice. And were your ma and da
there?

Ger Sure, Da's up to his oxters with the engraving for
The City Sports. You can hardly see him in the shop
for cups, medals and plaques. He seems cool as a
breeze about it all though. The Ma was there all right.
Sort of.

Debs How so?

Ger She's on new tablets now, so she's a bit spacy. You'd
want to have heard her, 'My first was a surprise, the
second was an accident and the third was a mistake.
You're starting where I finished.' Just as well Dee was
half comatose, she'd have hit her otherwise. It was
awful really. She didn't say a word to Connie the whole
time. Like it's all his fault.

Debs It takes two to tango, sure. She'll get over it, Ger.

Ger I wouldn't mind like, but the child is the head cut off
him.

Debs Ah God, I'm dying to see him. He sounds divine.
Have they any names picked out yet?

Marian flounces up to them. She's around the same age

and is wearing a pastel-coloured dress. She's in a complete dither.

How's it going?

Ger Hiya, Mars. Great news.

Marian Did ye see Barry at all? Did ye notice him going by? I'm hanging round ages but I must've missed him.

Ger As I was saying, great news.

Debs Dee had her baby at last.

Marian is hardly listening, looking up and down for any sign of her crush, Barry. Ger and Debs realize this but keep talking anyway.

Ger A boy. Eight pounds twelve ounces. She was in absolute agony for eleven hours and got sixteen stitches.

Debs And he's the dead spit of Connie.

Marian Still no sign of a ring I suppose. It's your poor mother's the one I feel sorry for.

Debs Don't be such a bloody crab-jaw, Marian. (*to Ger*) Listen to her.

Ger Congratulations must be gone out of style, is it?

Marian turns around quickly and tries to make herself as inconspicuous as possible, pulling her hair around her face and looking at the ground.

Marian Talk to me talk to me talk to me.

Debs What? What's wrong with you? Oh.

Debs wolf-whistles as Barry jogs on. He's seventeen, athletic-looking and dressed in running shorts and vest.

Ger Hey Bar, Barry, come here.

Marian Ger, stop, will you, you dirty louser. I'm going to wet myself if he comes over.

Barry trots over to them.

Hi, Barry.

47

Debs Give her a goozer. Go on. A big smackeroo.

Marian looks at her in shock.

Barry Huh?
Debs Ger. She's an auntie.
Ger Dee had a little boy.
Debs Nothing little about him, he's a big bruiser.
Barry Fantastic. A boy. That's fantastic.

He lifts Ger and twirls her around, kisses her on the cheek and sets her back down. Marian glares at Ger.

Is he like me? Ha ha. Only razzing, only razzing.
Debs You missed your chance there, Barry boy.
Barry Sure, what could I do when Connie was in like Flynn? I couldn't wipe his eye on him.
Ger Wouldn't Debs here do you grand, for the time being? We'd hate to see you stuck.
Debs As my mother says, never go out with someone better-looking than yourself. Give me a small and wiry fella any day.
Marian Every day'd be more like it.
Barry Ye're gas, girls. Listen, I better make tracks, gang. I'm on in the bar at six. The place is jointed below. I keep telling them you don't need drink to enjoy yourself but sure, what can you do?
Debs Ah, don't go, Bar, you're great fun.
Barry Give Dee my best, Ger. Tell her I'll try and get in during the week.

He trots off. Marian is practically swooning.

Ger He's an old dote, isn't he?
Debs A dote. And not a bit affected.
Marian Where's he working?
Debs Starrie's, part-time.
Marian Really? He's a hunk, his hair even. Oh, God, I'm

getting palpitations, I'm sure. Am I red?

Debs Pucey magenta.

Ger You're like a beacon. They should give you a job at Roches Point.

Debs Attention all shipping.

Marian That green powder's supposed to cover it. I'm going getting my money back.

Ger You're not puce at all, you're grand.

Marian What did his lips feel like, Ger?

Ger Would you stop. I wasn't taking pleasure in it. Sure, I'm spoken for.

Marian Did you see the legs on him?

Debs Wasted on a fella if you ask me.

Marian I hope he didn't see me blushing. Was he looking, do you think? Oh, God. I have a spot on my chin as well.

Debs and Ger make eyes at each other.

Debs Right so, I'm gone. I'll give you a ring or you ring me.

Ger See you later anyway. Number thirteen is sold, by the way.

Debs So I hear.

Marian About time. The place'd give you the creeps empty.

Ger goes into her house and Debs pushes off on the bike.

Debs Hop on and I'll give you a backer.

Marian Ah, not in a dress.

Debs Sure, who'll be looking at you? Get on.

Marian reluctantly gets on the back of the bike, tucking her dress under her.

Marian Drop me at the end of Lime Lawn. I'll walk from there.

49

Debs From there to where? You're not going to follow him down to Starrie's, are you.

Marian No. I'm just going to the shop.

Debs doesn't believe her and pulls at her eye. Marian shrugs.

Debs Good. I'd hate to see you making a show of yourself.

They cycle off.

SCENE TWO

The Martins' kitchen is sparsely decorated. What furniture there is is old and rickety. The only light is whatever natural light comes through the window. Dessie and Bridget are unpacking boxes and putting stuff away. Val is sweeping the floor and Pats is sitting apart.

Val (*to Pats*) What's wrong with you? What have you a face like a boiled shite on you for?

Pats shrugs and smirks.

Dessie Shut up, you, will you? Don't mind her, Pats.

Pats Sweep around me.

Val sweeps viciously, hitting the brush against Pats's legs. Pats doesn't budge.

Bridget Is he going getting the lights turned on in this house at all, I wonder? Can't hardly see your fist in front of you.

Dessie 'When there's a sun in the sky what kind of a fuckin' eejit'd be paying for electricity? D'ya think I'm made of money.'

Bridget and Pats smile nervously at his imitation of their father. Val goes for him with the brush, just stopping short of hitting him.

Val Listen to him, Dessie the big man. Don't start shaping you, I'm warning you, 'cause if he hears you he'll break your face for you. Don't come crying to me. Place is bad enough with her causing ructions the whole time. Look at her, the puss on her.

Pats I can't even remember what I'm supposed to have done this time, what big mortaler I'm supposed to have committed.

Bridget He's gone out shooting. I saw him taking the gun with him.

Dessie That's all he's interested in since Mam died. Blasting birds out of the sky.

Bridget That and that dog.

Bridget nods. Pats stands directly in front of Val.

Pats (*shouting*) What did I do? Tell me. Blink, is it? Is that it? No, no, maybe I looked crooked at something. Did I? Or did I walk or talk or breathe at the wrong time? Whatever it was, you probably told on me anyway, you apple shiner, you. Well, I'm sorry, all right, sorry for having been born. OK? Are you happy now? Are you? Yeah?

Val sneers at her, calmly puts the brush away and throws a sleeping bag at her.

Val There you are, make yourself at home, number three.

Bridget Ah, Val.

Val Ah, Val what? When she starts acting like a human being, she'll deserve to be treated like one.

Pats He has more mass on that dog than he has on me.

Dessie Than he has on all of us.

Val Maybe that's because the dog has more manners. Rough, isn't it? Ruff, ruff, ruff.

Bridget Dogs don't have manners, do they?

The sound of a banjaxed car pulling up interrupts them.

Dessie That's him.
Val Move. Quick. Watch yourself, number three, or you'll
be the one out in the shed next not Bran.

*Bridget, Dessie and Val leave the room. Pats throws the
sleeping bag on the floor.*

SCENE THREE

*Debs is sitting on the wall of the Martins' garden. Jimmy is
loitering awkwardly and Marian is peering in at the house.
Unseen by them, they are being watched by Val, Dessie,
Pats and Bridget.*

Marian Hey, look. The bathroom window is open.
Debs Mmm. Ger said she saw people going in and out all
right.
Marian What are they like?

Debs shrugs. Jimmy looks in idly.

Judging by the state of the place they couldn't have moved
in properly yet. No aerial up. Unless they don't have a
telly. I mean the garden even, it's still covered in nettles
and docks. No, they must've been just dropping off
some of their stuff. It's an awful eyesore, dragging down
the tone of the whole place.
Debs You'll have to go home when you want to go to the
jacks in future so, Jimmy.
Jimmy Wha?
Debs Wha?
Marian Don't tell me he went to the lav in the garden, did
he? That's disgusting, Jimmy.
Debs What are you talking about? We all did at some
stage. Oh, sorry, I forgot, you don't go to the toilet.
Marian You think you're smart, don't you?

Ger and her boyfriend, Mossie, rush out of her house.

Ger God almighty, I don't know which of them is worse, Ma or Aideen.

Mossie They're like balubas inside there. (*He takes out a single cigarette and lights it.*)

Jimmy Sneaky flash, Mossie.

Mossie Can't help it, boy. They come out of my pocket lighting and all.

Jimmy Oh, congrats are in order, Ger, I hear you're an auntie.

Ger Thank you, you're a gentleman, Jimmy. It's more than some people would say anyway.

Marian gives her a filthy look. Ger smiles back at her.

Jimmy If she's an auntie, what does that make you, Mossie?

Mossie Careful, Jimmy boy. Very careful.

Marian rolls her eyes. The others laugh. Ger playfully hits him.

Ger Chance would be a fine thing, wouldn't it, Mossie?

Mossie jumps up and grabs her and pretends to maul her.

Debs Look at him dropping the hand like that. Watch it, Ger, or you'll get the quick baby off of him.

Marian There's a lot of it about.

Ger Ah now, Mossie, don't be giving Jimmy an education he wouldn't know what to do with.

Jimmy Wha? Go away out of that, girl.

Marian They think they're hysterical.

Ger and Mossie are still messing when Aideen and Finn come out of the house arguing. Aideen has a big teddy under her arm.

Ger That was fast.

Aideen If she asks me have I news one more time, I'm telling you I'll never darken that door again. I'm serious, Finn.

Finn Ah, she didn't mean have you any news, just . . .

Aideen Well, what did she mean so?

Finn Like any news . . . any ska.

Aideen Same thing.

Finn Ah, Aideen love, you're getting hyper.

Aideen She's sick. The woman is sick, Finn. She has babies on the brain.

Finn Ah now. She's just . . .

Aideen What does 'Any bun in the oven?' mean so? That she's hungry?

Ger bursts out laughing. A dog starts to bark next door. Marian is the only one who notices, but Aideen remains the focus of her attention.

Marian Ahh, they have a dog.

Ger She didn't say that, did she? Jesus. It's the new tablets she's on, I'm sure.

Aideen I'll be on them myself next.

Finn Come on if you're coming.

Aideen We won't be staying long. We're going out for a meal tonight and the table is booked for . . .

Finn . . . half seven.

Aideen Half seven.

They walk off. Mossie makes a face after them. Ger rolls her eyes.

Mossie Though there's dough there, there's love there too though.

Ger Come on, you.

Mossie gets up reluctantly. Ger grabs him by the hand.

Come on with us, Debs. There's room isn't there, Finn? Wait till you see the baby. Just wait till you see him.

Debs Call in and tell my old lady I'm gone down to the hospital, would you, Mars?

Marian nods reluctantly.

Ta. You're a dote.

They troop off to Finn's car, leaving Marian and Jimmy.

Marian You don't fancy a walk down as far as Starrie's, do you?
Jimmy Wha? The pub? Sure I don't drink.
Marian That's not what I asked you.
Jimmy Oh. Oh, OK so.

Marian, worried that Jimmy thinks she fancies him, goes off in a huff.

Marian Forget it. It doesn't matter.

Jimmy shrugs and as he ambles off Pats comes out into the yard. She's as surprised to see Jimmy as he is to see her. Their eyes meet.

Jimmy Eh . . . hiya. How's it going?

Pats half smiles at him and looks away. She goes back indoors. He walks on.

SCENE FOUR

Connie, Mossie, Debs and Jimmy are playing football. Jimmy is useless. Jumpers and jackets are used as goal posts. Marian is sitting on the wall watching out for Barry. Ger knocks on the Martins' door. There's no answer. She comes out shaking her head and joins the others in the game.

Ger They must all be gone out.

Marian I told you I saw the car going off. Car, if that's the right word for it. Crock is more like it. I wouldn't be seen dead in it. The noise of it alone would make you die of mortification.

Debs God love you.

The play is fast, with lots of pushing and shoving. Whatever scores there are are accommodated within the dialogue.

Marian What do you want calling them out for anyway?

Ger Just to be friendly, Mars. Maybe they wouldn't be too uppity to play a game of ball either. You know, neighbourly. To say welcome to Lime Lawn and that.

Marian Well, they won't be unless they tidy up the place. It's in a chronic state.

Mossie Do y'hear her, the residents committee on legs.

Marian What would you know about it? You're not even from this park.

Connie Woo hoo, stand back, there's fighting talk.

Marian Well, as for you, we all know what you're like.

Debs Heavy sausage! I don't think we approve of Connie being a daddy, would I be right?

Marian I never said anything about that.

Ger Exactly.

Barry walks on and the ball is kicked to him. They all salute him.

Barry How are ye, gang?

Jimmy Just what we need. Fall in with us, Barry.

Barry Hey, congratulations, Connie boy. I wouldn't doubt you.

Connie You know yourself, Barry, beginner's luck.

He's a good player and the game takes on a new seriousness. Marian doesn't take her eyes off him. She's on the verge of joining in when Barry kicks the ball to

Jimmy, who kicks it miles wide and over the wall into the Martins' garden. His team groan and the others cheer. A dog starts barking. Connie picks up a jumper from the goal.

What's that, Jimmy?

Jimmy My jumper. Why?

Connie Duh. It's not your jumper, it's the goal. You gom.

Mossie Good man, Jimmy, as smart with your foot as you are with your mouth.

Connie Like his old man. You'll have no bother getting into the cops, Jimmy boy.

Jimmy Wha?

Ger Ah, leave him alone.

They start chanting:

All
Queenie, queenie, who has the ball,
Is he big or is he small,
Is he fat or is he thin,
Or is he like a safety pin?

Jimmy goes into the garden to retrieve the ball. As he does so Pats comes out and picks it up. She and Jimmy nod at each other.

Jimmy Oh . . . eh, hiya.

Debs How come they know each other?

Mossie I knew it all along, Jimmy Wha?, the dark horse.

They all move towards the garden.

Ger Hiya. I'm Ger from number twelve, next door there. I called in earlier to say hello and see if any of ye wanted to come out for a game. There was no answer. We thought ye must be out.

Pats is very conscious of everyone looking at her and doesn't say anything.

Debs I'll do the honours so. I'm Debs, from number four, and that's Connie, he's Mossie, that's Barry from number nine and Marian from number one, and you seem to know Jimmy already.

They all say hello and still Pats stands there. The dog continues to bark.

Ger And what's your name?
Pats (*whispers*) Pats.
Debs Huh? Sorry?
Jimmy Pats.
Ger Pats what?
Pats Martin.
Jimmy Martin.
Mossie You're on the ball there, Jimmy.
Connie For a change.
Ger So, do you want a game?
Pats Eh . . . no. I was only going out checking on the dog.

She's just passing the ball to Jimmy when Val comes out into the yard and snatches the ball. Dessie and Bridget appear behind her.

Val That's it. Game over, ball burst. Get inside, you.

Pats walks away. Dessie and Bridget disappear with her. Everybody stares at Val. She smirks at them and is about to go, taking the ball with her. Jimmy edges his way back towards the others.

Connie Ah go on, don't be lousy, give us out the ball.
Val That's the thing about balls, if you want them you should hang on to them.
Mossie What did I tell you, Con?

They start sniggering. Val glares at them.

Barry Sorry about that. Could we have our ball back please?

Val continues to glare at them. They stare back.

Val See enough? Do you? Well, you'll know me the next time you see me.

Debs Never a truer word was spoken.

Val I'd advise ye to scatter off from here and ye're not to be sitting on our wall either.

She walks off with the ball under her arm. The gang huddle together.

Mossie Mother of Jesus!

Connie What a wagon.

Ger That softened your cough for you now.

Marian What did your other one say their name is?

Jimmy Martin. Pats Martin.

Mossie Martian'd be more like it.

Connie Now you're sucking diesel.

Mossie starts to whistle and hum at the same time, making a sound like a spaceship.

Marian Where are they from, I wonder?

Mossie Mars! I hate to break it to you, but that's where Martians come from, Marian.

Connie The Flying Saucers gang, what do you think?

They laugh, except for Jimmy.

Mossie Brilliant, boy. The Flying Saucers.

Connie And she's the mother ship.

He makes the spaceship sound and the others join in.

Barry Quite a nice-looking girl if she did something with herself.

Marian puts a brave face on it.

Debs I'd say she's up all night all right, wondering what you think of her, Barry.

Ger Well said, Debs.

Mossie Well, that's the game shanghaied anyway. The go of Barry though, lads, 'Can we have our ball back please?'

Connie What a laugh. You sounded like you were eleven, boy.

Barry It was worth a try anyway. I'd love to stay now for ye to be slagging me, but some of us have to make a living.

Marian is up like a bullet after him.

Marian I'll walk down a bit of the ways.

Connie Me too. Your ma's not below in the hospital now, is she, Ger?

Ger You're dead safe, she's having a bit of a lie-down. Depression is exhausting apparently! I think I'll get it myself sometime.

The noise of Pats's father's car can be heard approaching and it shudders to a stop. Barry, Connie and Marian go off. Jimmy follows a little behind. Connie makes the spaceship noise and walks robotically as he passes the Martins' house. They all laugh.

Mossie Gas man, Connie.

Ger Mmm. No wonder the Ma is up to ninety though. He's no more than a kid himself sometimes.

Debs Sure Dee's a rock of sense, they'll be grand. Oh look, look. There's the father going in.

Ger The face on him. God almighty. He's like a mastiff.

Mossie Your one, the mother ship, didn't lick it up off the ground obviously.

Debs The younger one is like a mouse though.

Mossie There'll be some crack around here yet.

Ger Come on in for a coffee if ye want to. I'm on dinner duty again for a change. Waste of time like, no one eats it.

The three of them go into her house.

SCENE FIVE

In the Martins' kitchen Val, Dessie and Bridget are sitting at the table finishing their tea. Pats is also at the table but it's obvious that she hasn't eaten. They all seem very tense and are careful not to speak too loudly in case they're overheard. Val waves her hand in front of Pats's face and rubs her middle finger and thumb together.

Val Know what that is?

Pats just stares at her.

The smallest violin in the world.

Dessie This is demented. He should be had up.

Val She has no one to blame, only herself, drawing a gang of gurriers to the place.

Bridget They kicked the ball in. Sure, what did Pats do?

Dessie She was only checking on the dog, seeing what he was barking about, did you tell him that?

Pats Feed the dog. Exercise the dog. Watch the dog. The dog the dog the dog. Now I'm supposed to know what the dog is thinking even.

Val Ruff, ruff, ruff. All I know is Daddy heard them taking the piss out of him, whistling and laughing, when he was coming in. He asked me who they were and were we talking to them and I told him what happened. Full stop.

Bridget surreptitiously tries to pass Pats some food. Val sees her and grabs it back. Val's usual tight grip on the situation is beginning to crumble.

Fuck it anyway. I thought things'd be different in a new place.

Pats He couldn't stand the sight of me there, so why should he be able to stand me now?

Dessie He used to eat with us then at least.

Bridget She's ravenous, Val. What he won't know won't bother him.

Val And then I'll get it. He said she's not eating till she cops herself on and stops causing trouble and that's that.

Pats It's all right, Bridget, I'm watching my figure.

Dessie How would he find out if you weren't such an arse-licker?

Val If you want to get thumped, Dessie, that's your own business, just leave me out of it.

A loud bang comes from the floor above. Everybody sits stock still, staring at the table. The noise stops after four thuds.

Bridget (*whispers*) How many was it?

Dessie holds up four fingers. Bridget points to herself and the others nod. She looks terrified.

(*loudly*) Coming, Daddy.

She shoots out of her chair. Val puts her head in her hands. Dessie looks furious. Pats remains relatively detached. They listen to Bridget run upstairs and almost immediately back down. She makes a face in an attempt to indicate the level of the father's anger.

Daddy says you're to go up to him now.

Pats gets up slowly, takes a deep breath and gives a brave smile. Bridget takes a leather strap from a drawer or the back of the door and hands it to Pats.

(*mouthing*) Sorry, Pats.

Dessie (*whispers*) Oh, Jesus Christ, we're off.

Pats shrugs and starts laughing.

Pats Here we go loopy loo. (*She leaves, taking the leather strap with her.*)

Val Loopy loo is right.

*In silence and with military efficiency they clear the
table. The routine should seem well established, each
one having their own job. The slap of the leather strap
can be heard from upstairs. Pats cries out once. Dessie
kicks at the ground, otherwise nobody reacts or looks at
one another. Val puts a bowl of sugar, an open jar of
honey and an open pot of jam on the table. She marks
the level of their contents with a piece of Elastoplast
which Bridget cuts from a strip. Dessie fills a glass of
water and places it, unmarked, between the jam and the
honey. Bridget places the sleeping bag on the floor.
They go out in order of age, leaving the kitchen in
moonlight.*

SCENE SIX

*Pats is standing in the kitchen, whimpering like a pup. She
holds her dress away from the backs of her thighs, which
are criss-crossed with red stripes. She searches for a cool
surface to relieve her stinging legs. She takes the glass of
water and holds it to her thighs. Standing over the jam and
honey, she holds her hair out of the way and inhales the
smells, careful not to let her nose touch the contents. She
takes a tiny sip of water, savouring it and making it last as
long as possible, and takes another sniff of the jars which
seem to intoxicate her. Bringing the glass with her she
unzips the sleeping bag and lies down on it. Her legs chafe
against the surface. She silently yelps. She finishes the
water in one go, covers herself carefully and lies down to
sleep.*

*Ger, Debs, Jimmy and Marian are standing by the wall of
the hall at a disco. The lights are flashing and the music's
thumping but nobody is dancing yet.*

Debs Don't know what we keep coming to this for, there's
never any talent here.

Ger There is some here, OK, it's just that you've shifted all
of them.

*Barry comes in and Marian becomes very interested in
the floor.*

Barry How's the gang?

*They all salute him, glad to be associated with an older,
cooler person.*

No sign of Mossie, no? It's not all off, I hope. Only
slagging, Ger, only slagging.

Ger Naw, he's off with Connie somewhere. They're like
two parrots on a perch since the baby was born. They'll
get a right gonk when Dee comes home.

Jimmy Isn't he coming tonight?

Ger He said he'd see me inside.

Debs What's the point in jagging someone if they don't
pay in for you? That's what I think, anyway.

Barry isn't really interested. He's scanning the room.

Marian Were you working earlier?

Barry doesn't hear.

Barry Very few here. A lot must be away on hols, I
suppose. Well for some.

Jimmy Ah, it's early yet.

Barry Fair do's, Jimmy, ever hopeful. Might as well have a

look at the menu anyway. There's a few Spanish or is it
French students over there?

Debs Jimmy's holding out for one of the Flying Saucers,
aren't you, Jim?

Jimmy Wha?

Debs Wha? I saw you.

Barry They're only razzing you, boy. Catch you later,
gang. (*He moves off.*)

Marian Did you see the hairs on his chest, poking out of
his shirt?

Debs No chiffon scarf test for Barry, that's for sure.

Ger No test of any kind for Barry, I'm afraid.

Marian Oh, you're very pass-remarkable, aren't you?

Black-out.

    *Lights up and Ger, Debs, Barry, Marian and Jimmy are
dancing. Marian tries to edge closer to Barry, who dances
away every time. Jimmy is as good at dancing as he is at
football. Connie staggers in, followed by Mossie, who's
drunk as well, but not as bad. They're both holding
sparklers aloft. They dance over to the others, Connie
gives a sparkler to Jimmy. He obviously feels foolish with
it. Everybody shouts to be heard over the music.*

Ger Oh, Jesus. Cop on, will ye? If your man on the door
sees ye we'll all be out on our ear.

*Connie and Mossie are beyond caring and continue
dancing around the floor. Jimmy drops his sparkler and
leaves the dance floor.*

Barry The lads are in flying form, aren't they?

Debs So would you be if you had as much to drink as
they've had. Connie's palatic.

Ger So's Mossie. And he told me he had no money.
Bloody chancer.

Marian Who'd give him drink? He doesn't even look his
age, much less act it.

Ger Sure, they'd serve you in Flanagan's if you were wearing a nappy.

Debs One more pint and he'll need one.

Black-out.

Lights up and Jimmy and Marian are standing by the wall. She's forlorn-looking. Connie is asleep on the ground. Ger and Mossie are dancing slowly. He's hanging out of her, running his hands up and down her back under her top, her head is turned away to stop him kissing her.

Mossie What's wrong with you? You're not getting cranky now, are you?

Ger The smell of booze off you would knock a horse.

Marian catches Jimmy looking at her and pointedly looks away in case he was thinking of asking her to dance.

Mossie They've decided to call the baby Rory.

Ger I know. Dee told me earlier. I'm her sister, remember?

They continue to dance, Ger battling to stop him mauling her. She rolls her eyes at Marian.

Mossie What's up with you? Are you gone off me?

Ger gives him a filthy look and looks away at Connie, slumped on the ground.

Mossie You're very quiet. What are you thinking?

Ger Nothing. Absolutely nothing, Mossie.

Jimmy goes over to Marian. She shakes her head.

Marian No thanks.

Jimmy Wha? I was only going to say I'm going to head off.

Marian Why?

Jimmy The place is full of nothing, as usual.

Marian Right, see you so.

He leaves. She's very self-conscious, being left alone.

Mossie They're going to call the baby Rory.
Ger Go way. Really?

Black out.
   Ger is in the ladies' fixing her hair, etc., in the mirror,
when Debs comes in. The music can be heard in the
background. They talk to each other's reflections
through the mirror.

Ger You're gone ages. Who were you dancing with?
Debs Dancing me eye. I was out the back having a tongue
   sandwich.
Ger Oh, God. I thought you said there was no talent here.
Debs Well, thought made a fool of me. He's a lasher, girl.
Ger Brilliant. Well, who is he? Where's he from? And do
   we know his father?
Debs Eh, I haven't a clue what his name is but he's from
   Bishopstown.
Ger It's worse you're getting.
Debs Ah no, give us a break. He told me all right, only I
   couldn't hear what he said and I didn't want to be doing
   a Jimmy on it, saying What? the whole time.
Ger How old about?
Debs He's wearing aftershave anyway, so I'd say about
   sixteen.
Ger Mmmm. Lovely. Unless it's just his old man's.
Debs Stop. I'm sure I have a beard rash. It'd be lovely to
   be going with someone before going back to school, for
   the winter like.
Ger Get off with him first anyway.
Debs Ah, he's walking me home and all. You'd never go
   out and find out his name, would you, Ger? He's
   standing over by Connie. Make something up. Tell him
   I'll be out in a minute or something.

Ger Well, what does he look like?

Debs He's a vision.

Ger Shouldn't be hard to find so. Over by Connie?

Debs nods, Ger goes to leave, looks out into the hall and comes back into the loo.

I don't believe it. Mossie's conked out on the floor next to Connie. I'll kill him. I can't stand him when he's like that.

Marian rushes in past her. She's in an awful state. She looks at herself in the mirror and bursts into tears. The girls put their arms around her shoulders.

What's up with you?

Debs What happened? Is it Barry? It is, isn't it?

She nods. One of them gives her a tissue.

Marian I asked him up for ladies' choice, it was a fast one, and he just said thanks at the end of it and went back dancing with the Spanish one. Now he's after getting off with her. I saw them going out, with his arm around her and kissing her hand.

Ger Her hand?

Marian He doesn't even do Spanish, what'll he be able to say to her?

Debs If he wanted a conversation he'd have stayed at home with his mammy.

Ger She'd talk for Ireland.

Marian What am I going to do? Who am I going to ask to my Debs now?

Ger How do you mean your Debs?

Debs That's not for another four years.

Marian I know but I . . . love him. I swear. I really do. I love him. What am I going to do?

Debs Don't mind him. Sure, she'll be gone back in a few weeks.

Ger Yeah, Mars. You're too good for him.
Marian I'm not. Oh, God, what am I going to do?
Ger Do you want to go home? Come on, I'll walk down
with you. You'll be OK, Mars. Really, you'll be grand.

She leads her out with her arm around her shoulder.

See you tomorrow, Debs, or give me a ring or I'll ring you.

Debs kisses her hand. She and Ger smirk at each other.

Good luck with yer man, what's-his-name.
Debs What about Mossie?
Ger What about him?

Black-out.

SCENE EIGHT

*It's dark and Ger is walking home from the dance alone.
She's a bit pissed off. As she nears her house she hears a
noise. She stops and looks around, thinking it might be
Mossie following her.*

Ger (*whispers*) Mossie?

*There's nobody there. She walks on. There's another
noise. She steps into the shadows. Pats comes out of
Ger's house with some food in her hands. She's stuffing
bread into her mouth. It takes Ger a couple of seconds
to figure out who it is.*

Pats.

Pats stands still like a rabbit caught in headlights.

Pats Sorry.

*She drops the food and disappears into her own house.
Ger looks back and forth from Pats's house to the food.*

Gingerly she makes her way across the Martins' garden and peers in the kitchen window. It's difficult for her to see in. She can barely make out Pats on the ground in the sleeping bag. On the table are the pots of jam and honey and the sugar bowl as before. She comes back out of the garden. It's as if she wouldn't have believed it had happened but for the food on the ground. She picks it up, places it in the Martins' garden, then goes into her own house.

SCENE NINE

The sound of the father's car can be heard taking off, backfiring as it goes. Pats comes into the garden. She's more relaxed than usual, though she looks thin and undernourished. She's in the same clothes as always. Ger is coming back from the shops with newspapers, fruit and milk. She spots Pats and stands aside and watches her. Pats checks to see whether the food she dropped the previous night is still there. She finds it where Ger has left it. She scoffs it.

Ger Hey, Pats, what's going on?

Pats looks up, startled, and is about to run away.

Hang on. Hang on. I'll only follow you in. I saw your crowd going off in the car. It's all right, I won't bite.

Pats Going off to see our cousins. There wasn't room for me.

Ger So?

Pats I have to stay to watch the dog.

Ger You know well what I mean.

Ger's caring tone has Pats on the verge of tears. She stares at the ground.

Pats Sorry. Don't say nothing, sure you won't. I'll pay ye
back.

Ger Look, it doesn't matter, it was only a bit of bread and
jam and some fruit. Just my mother isn't great at the
moment, it's . . . well it's her nerves, my sister had . . .
ah, anyway, you know what I mean, and she'd have a
hernia if she came down and found someone in the
kitchen.

Pats We just ran out of shopping and I woke up in the
night ravenous. I was half sleepwalking, I'm sure. Don't
ask me what made me go . . .

Ger I looked in the window and saw stuff on the table
though.

Pats Gooseberry.

Ger Gooseberry?

Pats Gooseberry jam. That's all we have and . . . I hate
that. I hate it. If there's anything I hate in the whole
world it's gooseberries.

*Pats is getting desperate. It's clear Ger doesn't believe a
word Pats is saying, so she tries a different tack.*

Ger So how are you getting used to Lime Lawn? Do you
like it?

Pats Lime Lawn? Ehm . . . grand, grand. Where we were
before was in the middle of nowhere. The country. I like
seeing people around. There's more noise. Cars and
noise. Yeah.

Ger And did you sleep on the floor in your last house as
well?

*Pats looks at her, shocked that she knows. Jimmy comes
along.*

Jimmy How's it going?

Ger Oh, hiya, Jimmy. Well, you didn't last long last
night. (*to Pats*) A gang of us were up at Highfield. It's a
dance.

Jimmy A bit boring. No point in staying holding up the wall. None of the lads around, no?

Ger Probably down in the park airing their brains.

Jimmy I might take a wander down so, see what the crack is like.

Ger Why don't you go with him, Pats, see some of the local sights.

Pats and Jimmy What?

Ger Go on, why don't you?

Pats They don't . . . I've to be back before . . . I can't stay out, like.

Ger It's only down the road. Jimmy's very responsible. He'll make sure you're back on time. Won't you, Jim?

She takes some bananas from a bag and hands them to Pats.

Here, look, why don't ye have a bit of a picnic while you're at it? I'm all heart, aren't I?

Ger goes off into her house. Pats and Jimmy smile at each other and walk off in the other direction.

SCENE TEN

Pats and Jimmy are walking in the park. Initially he's very awkward, not sure of what to be saying to her. Pats is devouring the bananas. He watches her out of the corner of his eye.

Jimmy We used to have games of ball here before.

She continues to eat and drops the skins whenever she finishes one banana and starts another.

We're not let any more though.

She looks at him quickly as if to ask 'Why?'

They're minding the grass.

They stop. Jimmy squats. Pats eats.

So. So . . . eh, this is the park.

Pats looks around as if noticing it for the first time. She starts smiling.

Wha?

Pats The trees here look so . . . on purpose. That's all.

She sits on the ground next to him. She's still eating but getting very drowsy. His shyness is steadily evaporating.

Jimmy The pond froze over one winter and my dad saved a fella who went through the ice on his bike.

Pats Why?

Jimmy Eh . . . 'cause he was drowning.

Pats Why did he have to save him though?

Jimmy Eh . . . 'cause that's the sort of thing cops are supposed to do, I suppose.

She turns to look at him sharply. There's an awkward couple of seconds' silence. She can hardly maintain focus; her eyes are beginning to close. As she lies back on the ground, she stuffs another piece of banana in her mouth.

You must like them, do you?

Pats Not really.

She falls asleep. Jimmy looks at her and leans closer as if he's about to kiss her. He stops short of it, gets up and picks up her discarded banana skins. He returns and stands over her for a moment before putting the skins in his pocket. As he bends to wake her, he notices the marks on the back of her legs. He taps her very gently on the arm. She sits up immediately.

Jimmy You said you couldn't be out long. You had to go home.

Pats It's only a house.

He offers his hand and helps her up.

Jimmy The things on your legs there, are you after hurting them?

She pulls down her dress, is about to answer, stops, looks him dead in the eye and considers her reply.

Pats No. I didn't hurt them. (*She walks off ahead of him.*)

SCENE ELEVEN

Debs cycles on with Mossie on the back of the bike. He's holding his head.

Mossie Take it handy, will you, girl? My head is opening.

Debs Sorry, Mossie, we hadn't time to carpet the road for you.

He hops off the bike. Debs gets off and gives Mossie the bike to hold.

I'll give her a shout. Pull yourself together a bit, will you?

Debs goes into Ger's. He leans the bike against the wall, sits down and shakily lights a cigarette. He takes one puff of the cigarette. He nearly gets sick and tops it, putting the butt in his pocket. He's in bits. Debs comes back.

She'll be out in a tick. God, you're green.

Mossie So she went home with Marian, is it?

Debs Yeah.

Mossie And I was out for the count?

Debs Yeah.

Mossie I know we had a good laugh but I can't remember a bit of it. Did I go home with Connie?

Debs Don't know.

Mossie Where were you?

Debs I left soon after Ger went.

Mossie With who?

Debs I don't know.

Mossic Some tulips, the whole lot of us.

Debs I just don't know his name, I remember everything.

Mossie Don't go on about it, OK? My head feels like it's full of sand, all moving around from side to side. Never again. Still, it's not every day Connie's a da.

Debs It is from now on.

Ger comes out of the house in bad form and sits with them. She's holding something in her hand. It is an egg.

Look what I found.

Ger What? The wreck of the *Hesperus*. Lucky you.

Mossie Sorry for last night, Ger. I was out of order. Totally, like. You got home all right, anyway.

Ger No thanks to you.

Mossie I'm in the dog house, am I?

Ger looks at him tiredly. Mossie takes the butt from his pocket and lights it.

Debs Well, I had a gala if you must know.

Ger Oh, yeah, sorry. Did you? That's brilliant.

Debs I'm seeing him again Tuesday. Still don't know his name, like.

Ger Good. I'm delighted for you.

They sit for a while, saying nothing. Ger rocks the egg in her hand.

Debs What have you an egg with you for, Ger?

Ger takes a piece of paper from her pocket and passes it to Debs. She matter of factly holds up the egg.

Ger This is the latest from my mother. It's a baby! Good, huh?

Mossie What the . . . how do you mean, a baby?

Debs (*referring to the piece of paper*) This is like a timetable or something. Two o'clock, feed and change. Sleep for a while. Quarter past three, wakes crying. Possibly teething . . . This is bananas.

She passes the paper to Mossie.

Ger She says she's determined to teach me the responsibility involved in having a baby. She doesn't want me to end up like Dee.

Mossie Ah, for God's sake, it's an egg. What's she on about?

Ger She says she's not relying on the school any more to tell us anything. Her claim is that they teach us Irish for fourteen years and we come out not able to speak a word of it, so what kind of balls – sorry, that's not the word she used – hames are they going to make of sex education?

Debs I hate to admit it, but she does have a point there.

Mossie Yeah, but . . . that's bonkers, like. It's an egg.

Ger Not just any egg, Mossie, your egg.

She tries to give it to him.

Mossie Go away from me. Stop, will you?

Debs Ah, you should've had the old egg-cosy on, Mossie. That's what happens. Even I know that much.

Mossie The woman is totally off her game. Quit messing, Ger, take it away from me.

Ger Be careful, will you? It's the image of you and all.

Mossie This is giving me the creeps. Come on, you're making it up.

Ger No, look. (*She shows him the piece of paper.*) Is that my writing? Nope. It's my mother's. I'm not messing, honestly, Moss. And I have news for you, you're looking after it for the afternoon.

Mossie bursts out laughing. Ger pushes the egg at him and he pushes it away.

Laugh away, but I'm serious. Dee's coming home tomorrow and I have stuff to do.

Mossie Would you rev up, Ger. Come off it.

Ger That's the deal.

Debs According to this it . . . she, he, will be asleep for most of the afternoon, except for a bit of teething. Possibly.

Ger That's not that much responsibility now, is it? It's not like you'll be walking around with a pram.

Mossie But, Jesus Christ.

Debs Ah ah, not in front of the baby.

Mossie The Barrs are playing The Glen. I'm going to the game.

Ger So?

Mossie I am not going to the match with a fucking egg, do you hear me? Are you out of your mind?

Debs Tut tut, language, Mossie.

Ger Are you serious? You're not going to mind it?

Mossie Yes.

Ger Well, you better go so. Go off to your precious match.

Mossie Are you serious? You're not are you? You're only codding me. If it's over last night, I told you I was sorry.

Ger I'm serious, I said. Go on if you're going, otherwise give me a hand with this.

Mossie is backing away.

Mossie Fine, if you want to be like that about it.

Ger Yeah. Fine. See you. Good riddance to bad rubbish.

He goes off.

Debs Well, that shook him.

Ger Do him no harm to stew in his own juice for a bit.

Debs You were only messing, though? Testing him, like?

Ger Afraid not. You'd want to have heard the lecture I got. Dire, girl. There's nothing worse than your mother telling you about sex and things, sure there isn't.

Debs I know, it's chronic. If you pretend to be thick they tell you all sorts of gory mortifying stuff and if you act copped on then they think you're at it the whole time. (*She looks at the piece of paper.*) It's due for a feed and a change, Ger. Does she mean breast-feed?

Ger Are you out of your tree?

Debs What am I saying? It's an egg. God, I'm worse.

Ger Not that. But breast-feeding went out with the high bike.

Debs Oh . . . right. Well, I could baby-sit for you this afternoon if you like, I'm only washing my hair.

Ger Thanks anyway. I'll just put it in the fridge. It's only another one of the Ma's figaries, she'll forget about it.

Debs Here's Mars. I thought she'd still be mourning and weeping in the valley of tears.

Ger hides the egg and timetable.

Ger Say nothing to her about the other. I couldn't stomach her now.

Marian marches up to them, all business.

Marian I'm speechless. You won't believe what I'm just after seeing. Jimmy Wha? and your one from next door down in the park. Walking around, just the two of them, as if they were with each other, like. The cut of her. She looks like something dragged through a hedge backwards.

Ger Looks aren't everything, Mars, I thought you'd have figured that much out after last night.

Marian You mean Barry? Huh. I was telling my mother about it when I got in and she says he's heading the

78

same way as his father. I'm better off without him. Like
father like son, she said, a rag on every bush.

Debs Speak of the devil. Look at the walk of him. I ask
you.

Marian Jimmy had a lovely shirt on him actually. A kind
of a dark mauve. The colour really suits him.

*Barry comes on, delighted with himself. Marian isn't in
the least bit phased.*

Barry How are the girls?

Their greeting is subdued.

Fantastic night last night, girls, wasn't it? I'll tell you, I'm
knackered today, absolutely knackered.

Ger I better go in and give a hand. I'll see ye later on.

*Barry sits down next to Marian and Debs. Ger goes.
The sound of Pats's father's car arriving back. Debs
elbows Marian and they both get up.*

Debs We were just going ponemosing down the camino
actually, weren't we, Mars? See you around.

Barry Ponemos what? I'm not with you.

Debs Sorry, Barry, that's Spanish. I forgot you weren't
fluent.

Marian Adios, Barry. I'd get off that wall if I were you.
The Flying Saucers' da might get you.

Debs And mind the bushes.

Barry What are ye on about, girls? I can't keep up with
ye.

Marian We're only ragging you, Barry, only ragging.

They snigger and leave Barry looking a bit bewildered.

SCENE TWELVE

Pats is standing in the middle of their garden in a state of shock. Val, with her arms folded, is staring at her, fuming. Dessie and Bridget are ranging around the perimeters whistling and calling their dog, Bran. Their voices should seem a bit tired and hopeless, as if they've been at it for some time. All are worried-looking.

Val I don't get it. You can't do anything right. There's no hope for you, is there? And look at you, you don't give a sugar, do you? I don't blame him getting annoyed with you, you know that? I don't blame him.

Pats shrugs.

Did you check it? Did you check the shed door?

Pats It was closed last night, wasn't it? You'd swear I did it on purpose.

Val I wouldn't put it past you.

Pats Yeah, of course, Val, I love getting a walloping. If he wasn't hitting me, sure he'd take no notice of me at all. Then I'd really get worried that he didn't like me or something.

Val You're warped.

Pats He's the one who's warped. It's only a dog.

Dessie Leave her alone, Val, will you, for once. Pats, tell him he just bolted when you opened the door and you followed him down to the park but you couldn't catch him.

Val Tell him what lies you like, but someone's going to get a right kick up the arse over this and it's not going to be me, I'll tell you that for nothing.

Dessie Tell us something we don't know.

Bridget What'll we do if he gets a belt of a car? He hasn't a clue about traffic. I bet you he's in smush somewhere. You'll be murdered.

Pats Stop. (*whistles*) Here, Bran. Here, Bran Bran Bran.

Her voice trails off hopelessly. There are four loud knocks on the window.

Val Bridget. Quick.

Bridget goes into the house. The others look at each other. Jimmy comes on, puffed.

Jimmy No sign, not a glimmer. Why don't I do out a poster thing and hammer them up around the place and up in the shops and that? Will I? I'm not bad at it, like.

Val We don't need no help from the likes of you. It's our daddy's dog is missing. Clear off, why don't you, and mind your own business? It's her own fault.

Pats It's OK, Jimmy.

Dessie Thanks anyway.

Jimmy begins to slope away reluctantly. Bridget comes back out.

Bridget Pats, he wants you to bring up his cigarettes to him.

Silence. Jimmy looks on, trying to figure out what's going on.

Dessie In the name of fuck, the man's an animal. I've had it.

Pats slowly walks towards the house. Dessie runs in ahead of her. Bridget stands by Val, who puts her arm on her shoulder.

SCENE THIRTEEN

There's a big fuss outside Ger's house. Dee has arrived home. Aideen and Finn carry bundles of presents from the

*car into the house. Ger and Debs are admiring the baby in
Connie's arms. The dialogue is rapid fire and overlapping.*

Debs Ah, God. He's gorgeous, isn't he?

Connie Of course he is. Isn't he the spit of me?

Ger It's his nose gets me. It's brilliant, isn't it?

Aideen Mind he doesn't get cold, Connie. Pull up that
blanket around him.

Debs How's your ma? Is she still up to ninety over it?

Ger Herself and Dee are inside there laughing and crying
and hugging every second minute, so I presume it's roses
over the door again is it, Con?

Connie Ah, she's grand. She's calmed down again. I knew
once he was home . . . And you'd want to see the cot his
granddad made for him. Who's a lucky man?

Ger Yeah, imagine, that's what Dad was at the whole
time. Pretending to us he was engraving. He's a big
softie. Go on in and have a look at it.

*Debs goes inside. Jimmy comes along, followed by
Marian.*

Connie Well, what do ye think?

Marian Ah, look. Ah, look at him. Ah, God. The little
nails on him. Perfect. Hello, baby. Hello, Rory.

Jimmy Eh . . . yeah. He's grand, isn't he?

Aideen Come on in, Connie. That child will get his death
out there. He's used to the heat in the hospital.

Finn Do you hear the expert? You changed your tune
fairly fast.

Aideen It'd be no harm for you to take a few lessons from
Connie. You might need them someday.

Ger Come on in, let ye. There's lashings of sandwiches and
everything. They'll be curling up if they're not eaten.
Now, Mars, I should warn you, there's still no sign of a
ring.

Marian Go away out of that, don't be stupid.

They go into the house. Jimmy hangs back.

Ger Jimmy?

Jimmy Eh . . . Mossie asked me to call up to see what the lie of the land was.

Ger Oh, did he now? And what are you going to tell him?

Jimmy You tell me.

Ger Tell him he should have the guts to do his own dirty work and not have you running his messages for him.

Jimmy I was out anyway, looking for the dog.

Ger Huh?

Jimmy Yeah, Bran Martin got out when myself and Pats went down to the park yesterday. Remember you said to her to go down with me? Now he's lost.

Ger Yeah and?

Jimmy Well, I think she got into fierce trouble over it because she was meant to be minding him. She seems to be picked on the whole time. I was out half the night looking for him. I'm not sure what's going on, like, but I'd say their da is ferocious if the sister is anything to go by.

Ger Did you call in?

Jimmy The sister told me to clear off and I don't want to make things any worse. They're all very cagey in front of her for some reason.

Ger Mmm. There's something fairly odd going on there all right. Did Pats say anything to you?

Jimmy She hardly opened her mouth. She just ate all the bananas you gave us.

Ger Like she was starving?

Jimmy I thought that was a joke, like. The picnic and that. Then she fell asleep sitting on the grass. Only for a few minutes. She seems real shy, very nice though.

Ger Oh, God, I don't know.

Jimmy The brother seems nice enough as well. I mean, I know it's their da's dog, but still.

Ger If you hang on a while I'll go in with you. I can't this minute 'cause of the baby and that. I don't want to be spoiling things. There's loads of grub inside.
Jimmy I should call over to Mossie, he'll be wondering.
Ger Sure, give him a buzz from my place.
Jimmy OK so. Your ma won't mind?
Ger Naw, she won't even notice.

They go inside.

SCENE FOURTEEN

Pats is sitting at the kitchen table. She's got three cigarette burns on her cheek. Dessie comes in. He has a black eye. They are both very jittery. A shotgun is leaning against the wall. He sits at the table and opens his hands. He's holding six shotgun cartridges. They both stare at them for a minute.

Pats But that's loads. Where did you get them?
Dessie I was putting them by . . . for a rainy day.
Pats Dessie, look, he said he was sorry . . . maybe he won't . . .
Dessie And you believe that bollox?
Pats I'm sorry you got it too, you shouldn't have stood up for me. I told you. What are we going to do if they have Bran with them when they come back?
Dessie Don't, Pats. Stop it. Don't back out on me now. You swore.
Pats He just lost his temper. I should've checked the shed. I know. I can't put a foot right. I can't help it. It's my own fault.
Dessie Stop it, Pats. He'll never burn you or me or anyone else again. Do you hear me? I want to see him die roaring.

Pats No. No, just only hurt him. Look that's what we
said. Hurt him.

Dessie All right, all right. I know what we said.

Pats Maybe we should wait till he's better, till he's over his
cold.

There's a knock on the window.

It's them. Jesus Christ, hide the bullets.

*Dessie panics and fumbles, dropping the cartridges.
They both scramble to pick them up, forgetting to hide
the gun. Ger and Jimmy walk into the kitchen. Pats and
Dessie pocket the cartridges.*

Ger Hi. Sorry for barging in. We knocked. We heard
voices so we knew someone was home.

*She looks at Jimmy for help but he just nods. He's
staring at Pats's face. She covers it with her hand.*

Eh . . . anyway. We're, eh, having a bit of a do inside, my
sister just had a baby, and, em, well, come in if ye'd like
to. It's only the neighbours and ourselves, nothing
grand. Ye're welcome.

There's an awkward silence.

Dessie Thanks. Thanks, OK.

Jimmy What happened to your face?

Pats Huh?

Jimmy Your face. What's that from?

Pats (*suddenly bright*) How do you mean? Oh, that.
That's just . . . ah nothing. It's midge bites. Yeah.

Jimmy Midge bites?

Ger It doesn't look like it to me. It looks more like . . .

Pats There. On my face you mean? Oh, they're spots. I'm
always at them, aren't I, Des? I know sure, I'm like a
curranty scone, aren't I? I can't help it. I must be picking
them in my sleep even.

Ger When you're asleep on the floor even?

Pats Go away. That was only once. For privacy.

Jimmy The same way that they're spots on the back of your legs, I suppose?

Pats What are you talking about? I said I didn't hurt them.

Jimmy Exactly. You didn't. But who did? I'm not that stupid.

Pats I don't know what you're saying. It's just from the chair or something.

Dessie Shut up, Pats, stop making excuses for him.

Jimmy We heard ye talking before we came in.

Ger Look, ye'll only get in worse trouble if ye start shooting people. We heard ye. It sounds mad even to be saying it. Shooting people, God. If your dad is . . .

Pats We were only messing, weren't we, Dessie? For God's sake.

Dessie takes the cartridges out of his pocket and puts them on the table. He holds out his hand and Pats puts her cartridges into it. He puts them on the table too.

Dessie We weren't. I wanted to blast that bastard sky high.

Pats We were only going to injure him a bit. Just a small bit. (*She starts to cry.*) More like a fright. It's my own fault 'cause I wouldn't cry.

Ger picks up the cartridges and gives them to Jimmy. Dessie puts his arms around Pats. They cling to each other, sobbing.

Ger Don't worry. It'll be all sorted out.

Dessie What's going to happen now? They're due back in a while.

Jimmy I'll give these to my dad and tell him the story.

Pats is half laughing, half crying.

Pats But I didn't go through the ice on a bike. Don't bring
the guards up. He'll kill me. Please, I beg of you. He
will, I swear.

Ger Listen, no one's going killing anyone.

Dessie They'll believe us, Pats. Sure, what would we be
making it up for. Look at the state of the two of us even.

Ger Did he do that to your eye too?

Dessie nods.

Pats Are you sure? Promise.

Jimmy Ah no. They'll believe you all right. My dad's
sound like that. Honestly.

Ger Do ye want to come into my place till . . . well, you
know?

Dessie We'll hang on here if that's all right.

Ger You're sure you've no more of those things for the gun?

Dessie shakes his head.

You better put it away anyway. In case he comes home
before . . .

Jimmy I'll go down and get my dad now, OK?

Ger Are you sure you don't want us to stay with ye?

Pats No. Thanks anyway. We'll be grand.

Dessie Yeah. We'll be grand.

Jimmy Yeah.

Ger and Jimmy leave.

SCENE FIFTEEN

Ger and Jimmy are standing on the road.

Ger God, it's unbelievable, isn't it? What's going on?
Imagine if they shot him. God almighty.

Jimmy I knew there was something weird going on but . . .

87

Ger I'll be inside if your da wants to talk or anything. Are we witnesses now? I hope we don't have to stand up in court or anything.

Jimmy I don't know, I doubt it. Just lucky we heard them in time, I suppose.

Ger Right. I'll go on in. I won't say anything – you know, with the party going on and all – but call in if you need me.

Jimmy I'll let you know what's happening. Thanks, Ger.

As he leaves, Mossie comes on, very sheepish-looking, with something behind his back.

Mossie Thanks for the phone call, Jimmy boy.

Jimmy Oh, yeah. You're welcome.

Ger Well, well, well. What a surprise.

Mossie Look, Ger. Sorry, all right? I know I was acting the gom. I should've copped that it was your ma's idea and . . . ah, I'm useless at saying stuff like this, but here, I bought you a present.

He takes the parcel from behind his back. It's roughly wrapped in plain paper.

Ger Look, Mossie, I'm not in the humour for you now. There's all sorts of shenanigans going on and I have enough on my plate.

He holds out the parcel. Ger takes it resignedly and shakes it.

What is it?

Mossie I wouldn't rattle it too hard. Open it, go on.

She tears off the paper. Inside is a half-dozen eggs. She bursts out laughing.

Ger Ah, Mossie. You eejit. I never knew you were such a romantic.

She puts the eggs down and they kiss. While they're kissing, Barry and Jimmy run on.

Jimmy Quick, quickly ring an ambulance. There's been a crash.
Ger Where?
Jimmy At the corner. Oh, God.
Barry It's The Flying Saucers' car.
Ger Jesus, Mary and Joseph, I don't believe you. Their car. Crashed into what?
Barry It's wrapped around the telegraph pole below by the traffic lights.
Jimmy Quick. Can I use your phone?
Ger Yeah, sure, come on.

They go into the house.

Barry The bloody madman. He swerved to avoid a dog that ran out in front of him. Completely mad. He had nowhere to go.
Mossie Is it bad?
Barry Oh, yeah. Serious, I'd say.

They follow into the house.

SCENE SIXTEEN

In the Martins' kitchen Val, Dessie, Pats and Bridget are sitting around the table eating. There is a new serenity about them.

Val Are you OK? Do you want more?
Pats I'm fine.
Dessie I will, if it's there.
Bridget Aren't you finishing that?
Pats No, have it.
Val Finish it.

Pats Really, I'm full.

*There's a knock at the door. Bridget freezes as usual,
then relaxes once she realizes it's the door.*

That's probably Jimmy for me.
Bridget Where are you going?
Pats Just down as far as the park for some air.
Val Be back by half-five, will you? Auntie Kay is coming
for us and we need to get cleaned up and that.
Pats I'll be back.

Black-out.

SCENE SEVENTEEN

A church bell rings. Lights up.
   *Graveyard. Dessie, Pats, Val and Bridget are standing
around the grave. The rest of the cast are behind,
mourners at The Flying Saucers' father's funeral.
Everybody is solemn-looking, as if listening to a priest.
Bridget steps forward and throws earth on the coffin. Val
follows suit. Dessie steps forward and slowly lets the earth
fall from his hand. Pats closes her eyes and steels herself to
step forward. She does so and flings her handful of earth
at the coffin. A dog barks in the distance. There is silence
for a couple of seconds, then Pats starts to laugh, followed
by Dessie and Bridget, then Val. Their laughter is
infectious and is picked up by Ger and Jimmy and so on,
until the entire congregation are hysterical.*

Online Resources for Secondary Schools and Colleges

To support the use of Connections plays in the Drama studio and the English classroom, extensive resources are available exclusively online. The material aims not only to make the most of new technologies, but also to be accessible and easy to use.

Visit *www.connectionsplays.co.uk* for activities exploring each of the plays in a wide range of categories:

- Speaking and Listening
- Writing
- Reading and Response
- Practical Drama
- Plays in Production
- Themes

Carefully tailored tasks – whether for KS3, KS4 or A Level – are accompanied by clear learning objectives; National Curriculum links; ideas for extension and development, and for differentiation; Internet links; and assessment opportunities.

The material has been compiled by a team of practising English and Drama teachers, headed by Andy Kempe, author of *The GCSE Drama Coursebook* and (with Lionel Warner) *Starting with Scripts: Dramatic Literature for Key Stages 3 & 4*.

STANLEY THORNES